STEPHEN D. KERTESZ, the author, is Charles
Miles Professor of Political Science at the
University of Notre Dame, where he is also
Director of the Soviet and East European,
and West European Programs, and Chairman
of the Committee on International Relations.
Dr. Kertesz has been a Guggenheim Fellow,
is Contributing Editor of *Current History*
and Advisory Editor of *Review of Politics*,
and has published, among other volumes,
*Diplomacy in a Whirlpool: Hungary
Between Nazi Germany and Soviet Russia;
Diplomacy in a Changing World* (with
M. A. Fitzsimons) ; *American Diplomacy in a
New Era;* and *East Central Europe and the
World: Developments in the Post-Stalin Era.*

STEPHEN D. KERTESZ

The Quest for Peace
Through Diplomacy

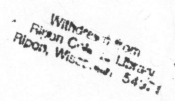

A SPECTRUM BOOK

Prentice-Hall, Inc., Englewood Cliffs, N.J.

To Peter, Christine, and Michael
and their contemporaries in the twenty-first century

Library of Congress Catalog Card Number
67-23503.

Printed in the United States of America.

Current printing (last number):
10 9 8 7 6 5 4 3 2 1

Preface

The present work and a forthcoming extended version are the result of research, teaching, and experience in diplomacy. Recently, three trips to most of the West European countries, including numerous visits to headquarters of international institutions, foreign offices, and embassies, have facilitated my study of new diplomatic methods and national attitudes of the West European and North American governments. Despite the increasing togetherness of the world, it seems that the outmoded ideas of sovereignty and nationalism have remained, and even international organizations have developed special atmospheres and interests. National societies and international organizations consider the world from their own points of view, accept or develop diplomatic methods suitable to their real or imagined interests and idiosyncrasies, and incline to ignore other approaches. It is my hope that the discussion of rapidly developing diplomatic diversities in the same volume will contribute to the understanding of what diplomacy is, and can or cannot do, today.

It would have been possible to limit the topic of this volume to procedures of diplomacy, but such a discourse would have satisfied only a limited number of specialists. Diplomacy does not operate in a vacuum; it would not be helpful to discuss techniques without mentioning the theater where diplomacy operates and some of the dilemmas diplomats have to face. Patterns of international institutions and historical relations are relevant to diplomacy, and so are social, economic, and military developments. As for political and institutional problems, they will be treated only with the brevity necessary to put into focus the theme of the volume.

I would like to express my thanks to the many civil servants, international officials, diplomats, and statesmen who helped me as well as to the Guggenheim Foundation, the Rockefeller Foundation, and the University of Notre Dame. It would not be proper to mention the names of national and international civil servants who read passages of my manuscript, freely expressed their views, and made suggestions. I am deeply indebted to them. Also to my fellow academicians with whom I debated numerous topics relevant to my study. John Goormaghtigh, Director of the European office of the Carnegie Foundation; John C. Campbell, Director of Political Studies at the Council on Foreign Relations; Philip E. Mosely, Director of the European Institute at Columbia University; Harold K. Jacobson, Professor of Political Science at the University of Michigan; George L. Kline, Professor of Philosophy at Bryn Mawr College; and George A. Brinkley, Professor of Government and International Studies at the University of Notre Dame, read the manuscript, entirely or partly, and shared their thoughts. Some expressed disagreements and even differences in political philosophy. Their comments stimulated my own thinking. I owe particular gratitude to two close friends, Robert H. Ferrell, Professor of History at Indiana University, and M. A. Fitzsimons, Editor of the *Review of Politics*. They participated in my labor and read the various versions of my manuscript; their criticisms, suggestions, and editorial advice were most helpful. Dr. Theodore Ivanus of the Notre Dame Library cheerfully provided me with source material and verified many references. For the final version of my manuscript my research assistant, James Maney, checked the footnotes. Dennis T. Breunan compiled the index.

The author also wishes to acknowledge the gracious permission of *Foreign Affairs* to reprint, in Chapter Five of this book, two passages by Dean Rusk from "The President," in *Foreign Affairs,* Vol. XXXVIII, No. 3 (April 1960), pages 365 and 369. This material is copyright © 1960 by the Council on Foreign Relations, Inc.

Amidst rapidly changing diplomatic problems and after the rough-and-tumble of European capitals, it was a welcome change for me to abandon the dizzying tempo of our time and formulate my conclusions *procul negotiis* in the serene atmosphere of the Rockefeller Foundation's Villa Serbelloni at Lake Como. The surrounding mountains have witnessed the invasion as well as defeat of many conquerors, the glories and disappearance of the North Italian city states. The idyllic atmosphere of the Villa, haunted by historical memories, somehow fostered both a sense of detachment and humility. The harmony and natural beauty of this stimulating place was conducive to quiet thinking.

S. D. K.

Contents

Abbreviations

ACC	Administrative Committee on Coordination
ANZUS	Australia, New Zealand and United States Security Treaty
BENELUX	Belgium, Netherlands and Luxembourg
CENTO	Central Treaty Organization
Cominform	Communist Information Bureau
Comintern	Communist International
DAC	Development Assistance Committee
DAG	Development Assistance Group
ECA	Economic Commission for Africa
ECAFE	Economic Commission for Asia and the Far East
ECE	Economic Commission for Europe
ECLA	Economic Commission for Latin America
ECOSOC	Economic and Social Council of the United Nations
ECSC	European Coal and Steel Community
EDC	European Defense Community
EEC	European Economic Community
EFTA	European Free Trade Association
EPU	European Payments Union
ERP	European Recovery Program
EURATOM	European Atomic Energy Community
FAO	Food and Agriculture Organization
GATT	General Agreement on Tariffs and Trade
IAEA	International Atomic Energy Agency
IBRD	International Bank for Reconstruction and Development
ICAO	International Civil Aviation Organization
ICITO	Interim Commission for the International Trade Organization
IDA	International Development Association
IFC	International Finance Corporation
ILO	International Labor Organization
IMCO	Inter-Governmental Maritime Consultative Organization
IMF	International Monetary Fund
ITU	International Telecommunication Union
Little Europe	Member states of EEC
MLF	Multilateral Nuclear Force
NATO	North Atlantic Treaty Organization
NDAC	Nuclear Defense Affairs Committee

NPG	Nuclear Planning Group
OAS	Organization of American States
OECD	Organization for Economic Cooperation and Development
OEEC	Organization for European Economic Cooperation
SACEUR	Supreme Allied Commander Europe
SEATO	South East Asia Treaty Organization
SHAPE	Supreme Headquarters Allied Powers Europe
The Six	Member states of EEC
UN	United Nations
UNCTAD	United Nations Conference on Trade and Development
UNIDO	United Nations Organization for Industrial Development
UNDP	United Nations Development Program
UNESCO	United Nations Educational, Scientific and Cultural Organization
UNICEF	United Nations International Children's Emergency Fund
UNRWA	United Nations Relief and Works Agency for Palestine Refugees
UPU	Universal Postal Union
US	United States
USSR	Union of Soviet Socialist Republics
WEU	Western European Union
WHO	World Health Organization
WMO	World Meteorological Organization
World Bank	International Bank for Reconstruction and Development

ONE

Introduction

Diplomacy today is a complicated and hazardous undertaking, yet it is also a highly necessary one. Although the meaning of diplomacy is different on the opposite sides of the iron, bamboo, and other curtains, at the present juncture of history only the instruments of diplomacy, properly understood and carefully used, can protect mankind against devastating wars. Unprecedented advances in weapons technology have given each of the superpowers the ability to destroy the human race, and similar capabilities are gradually being acquired by several of the lesser powers.

In this dangerous world environment, diplomacy has to overcome enormous difficulties. Like the search for the Holy Grail it involves not merely perilous but long and patient labors. With the rapid growth of scientific knowledge and technology, mankind is now able to establish an affluent and peaceful world. But this golden age can only come about after a long evolutionary process, during which civilization may possibly be destroyed.

It is not merely peace which mankind is seeking to achieve: for the foreseeable future the attainment of world security must form a part of a long and comprehensive reforming of political, social, and legal institutions, many of which are no longer in harmony with the demands of our technological age. Under existing world conditions, political wisdom has little leverage; events are out of hand; technology has taken charge in many developed countries. People accept changes in gadgets much more readily than in politics because they realize the usefulness of technical invention. People are reluctant to accept new ideas, political processes, or forms of living, especially when these concern the organization and actions of societies. The desirable transformation of the social and political order is an extremely slow process. This is particularly true of relations among states.

I

To transform the political organization of mankind, so that it is adapted to great changes of the world, will require a considerable time. During this period of transition the aim of diplomacy should be to prevent conflicts which might cause irreparable damage.

There are a great many peace societies and movements which seek to define the bases of peace among nations; they flourish mainly in countries which protect and promote intellectual freedom and permit political participation of citizens in thought and action. There is a sincere longing for peace in communist-dominated countries. But because of lack of freedom of association and speech, no genuine peace movement can emerge there. Communist peace campaigns are an instrument of Party policy. Nikita Khrushchev repeatedly announced that his program of peaceful coexistence included support for "wars of national liberation," and his successors have reaffirmed this pledge. In this spirit Aleksei N. Kosygin emphasized in an interview with James Reston of the *New York Times* on December 7, 1965, that "wars of national liberation are just wars." If the Soviet Union declares an aggression a holy war of "national liberation," the United Nations could not act under Chapter VII of the Charter because of Soviet veto. While Soviet representatives advocate national liberation, the USSR has imposed an oppressive communist system on more than a hundred million people in Eastern Europe. When the Hungarians wanted to regain their national independence in 1956, the Soviet Union intervened militarily.

Despite the fact that in recent years the United States has concluded several agreements of importance with the Soviet Union, which have improved US-USSR relations, a genuine thaw between communist and Western countries may be Western wishful thinking, as it was repeatedly in the past. Critical issues of the cold war remain unresolved. China advocates a militant policy; the Soviet Union is unyielding, if more cautious. The precarious existence of many inexperienced new states is a source of diplomatic complications and unforeseeable developments.

One often hears that ideological and political differences between the Soviet Union and China, and other changes within the communist world, mean that we are on the threshold of fundamental transformations. This suggestion is true in the sense that political systems based on Marxism-Leninism proved inadequate in important segments of domestic affairs and foreign relations. If communist doctrines had the validity that thousand of pages of Marxist-Leninist writings seek to demonstrate, then internal conflicts within the communist family of nations could not have taken place. Despite the bankruptcy of communist doctrines, the leading communist empires still use Marxist slogans to justify their totalitarian regimes and expansionist and subversive foreign policies. For communist leaders, expansion of communism remains an *a priori* assumption, an article of faith, part of the historical process. The cold war is a product of communist policies. After World War II the West did not introduce ideology to international relations. It was not in the Western interest to develop differences with communists into a sort of religious war; elimination of ideological factors from international policies would be advantageous to all nations. But no farsighted diplomacy can ignore the conflicting philosophies of Western and communist governments. Although Moscow no longer controls the communist world, and relations between some communist countries and the West are changing, endeavors to create more friendly relations with communist states should not disregard the strong ideological commitment of the communist leaders. As long as Marxist-Leninist ideology constitutes the political frame of their thinking, proposals for a universal society of mankind and a worldwide rule of law remain unrealistic.

Western strength and a prudent use of the instruments of diplomacy may persuade communist leaders to accept a relaxation of tensions as a desirable accommodation rather than as a temporary tactic. It is a primary obligation of Western diplomacy to establish conditions under which subversion and aggression cannot succeed. As long as division is imposed on Europe and free exchange of ideas between nations is not permitted, mankind is far from a genuine peace. Dictatorships are not under popular control; their actions may suddenly create crises. Even if the contemporary ideological rift should subside, the rise of new aggressive ideologies is always a possibility.

In this volume I have attempted to examine some of the intricacies of the search for peace through diplomacy. First, I discuss the present arena of international politics and the purpose and methods of diplomacy. Because thinking in political matters has undergone little change during the centuries of recorded history, the second chapter briefly reviews past developments relevant to contemporary diplomacy. The third chapter deals with the adaptation of diplomacy to some of the vast changes since World War I. Chapters Four to Eleven discuss major contemporary transformations, the new forums and methods, the power and limits of diplomacy, and the world task of Western diplomacy.

The arena of the United Nations reflects the complexities of the contemporary world. The General Assembly has become a forum of public diplomacy—a function fulfilled by the League of Nations between the world wars. Both the League and the United Nations provided new opportunities and new channels for diplomacy. The League failed because its objectives and means were not in harmony with political realities, but the chasm between the lofty principles and universalist concepts of the United Nations and the existing international conditions is even larger. The world organization can make little progress toward peace because many member states are unwilling to act for world interests. The heterogeneous nature of the contemporary state system, the contradictory objectives of leading states, rampant nationalism—all these are obstacles. In the shadow of Armageddon the United Nations is a convenient forum for settlement of some issues or at least for peace-saving formulas in delicate situations. Meanwhile the regional and functional organizations might create security zones and bring friendly cooperation in some areas. Here NATO is of importance. It checked the Soviet advance in Europe. Its success and the new strength of Western Europe have released forces that might require the reconsideration of policies, diplomatic arrangements, and international institutions. Western Europe since 1945 has produced a great variety of international organizations. The economic, social, and technical international bodies have developed new methods and techniques—that is, a special diplomacy for solution of problems in the society of states.

Proliferation of world, regional, and technical international organizations might become a source of new problems. Political leaders often live in an atmosphere of wishful thinking, disposed to believe—or at any rate to pretend—that creation of a new international agency leads toward the solution of some problem. In practice the functions of new international bodies may overlap those of existing organizations, aggravating problems of coordination. Novel institutions and organizational changes may generate illusions but they are not substitutes for agreement, and might even camouflage conflicting policies for a time, in reality only transferring unsolved problems and disagreements to different spheres.

Functional international organizations may be useful, but political walls limit their activities. Progress is doubtful as long as world powers are unwilling to accept reasonable methods for peaceful change and for pacific settlement of international disputes. The ideological gulf between major powers constitutes a formidable obstacle for progress in this direction. Without an understanding of common problems and the acceptance of a worldwide rule of law, mankind may approach journey's end.

The cumulative effect of the great discrepancy between the development of the social and the natural sciences, and the simultaneous cleavage in goals, ideology, and methods between communist and noncommunist states, and the multiplication of new and in many ways inexperienced states has created a precarious situation for the human race and has immensely complicated the task of policy-makers and diplomats. Modern weapons, modern means of transportation and communication, and effective methods of indoctrination open new possibilities for dictators. Fascist, Nazi, and communist dictatorships have demonstrated that a few determined individuals can exercise tight control over many, and that such a rule can eventually be established and consolidated even over vast regions. Moreover, the secret formulation and execution of foreign policy is much easier in dictatorships than in democracies. Dictators enjoy many short-run advantages—and because of the destructive capability of contemporary weapons today the short-run may be decisive. This situation is a source of constant danger to mankind.

One might add that if communism were to disappear overnight, the international problems of the contemporary world would remain baffling. Western and communist political mistakes frequently have originated in lack of understanding of the strength of the new political and social forces in this changing world. The temptation is for Western political leaders to blame communist machinations for Western failures. Such a view gives to communism greater strength than it has, and shows its leaders to be more shrewd than they are. Because of the communist threat, adherents to some schools of thought have viewed the contemporary world crisis almost exclusively as a struggle between communist and noncommunist states. This perspective is too narrow; it omits the fact of nationalism, which is almost universally rampant. New social forces are reshaping the thoughts of men about themselves and the rest of the world. The eagerness of Makarios, Archbishop and President of Cyprus, to accept communist assistance for nationalistic reasons is an example of the diplomatic complexities of our time.

Traditional diplomacy had the advantage of working with a broad consensus within a narrow circle. As long as this situation prevailed, diplomacy could be identified with negotiations, as did Harold Nicolson in his celebrated book, *Diplomacy*. But this identification no longer corresponds to realities in international relations. Conditions in the twentieth century have created, necessarily, a diplomacy different from that of the nineteenth century. In the strict sense, diplomacy remains the execution of foreign policy through government agencies. According to broader definition, diplomacy means the conduct of foreign relations between politically independent entities—through bilateral negotiation, multilateral conference, international organization. But pedantic distinctions between diplomacy and foreign policy are not helpful. Many government agencies participate in the formulation and execution of foreign policy, and there is the special diplomacy of international organizations. Diplomats themselves not only carry out government decisions but through their reports and recommendations participate in making foreign policy. While diplomacy in part deals with maxims and tactics that inevitably arise from the process of negotiation, diplomacy is but a part of a great context which embraces social forces, institutions, and values, including ideology. It is indeed impossible to evaluate diplomatic methods, techniques, and organizational problems without considering the basic issues of foreign policy. And the choice of methods and procedural matters may on occasion be as important as basic policy.

Diplomacy has responded in some considerable measure to the formidable challenges of the twentieth century. Its scope has broadened, and new diplomatic methods and techniques have extended into novel fields in the changed political arena of world affairs. In the expanding world community diplomatic approaches and procedures have greatly diversified; the importance of economic and scientific problems has been recognized, and the role of specialists has increased; international agencies have become new theaters for diplomatic activity; parliamentary diplomacy, and the publicity connected with it, has changed many aspects of diplomacy.

Contemporary diplomacy in all its ramifications may be grouped under the following categories:

1. Contact and negotiation through usual *bilateral diplomatic channels.*

2. A great variety of *ad hoc international conferences,* including political gatherings of the highest representatives of leading powers—so-called summit meetings.

3. *Consultative diplomacy* of permanent collective bodies, such as NATO and other regional organizations.

4. *New forms and tools of diplomacy, developed by the specialized agencies* and other functional organizations.

5. Open diplomacy by conference as introduced by the League of Nations and developed by the United Nations, which has appropriately been called *parliamentary diplomacy.*

6. Apart from parliamentary diplomacy, the *diplomacy of parliamentarians* has appeared in some international assemblies, such as the Consultative Assembly of the Council of Europe, the European Parliament, the Assembly of the Western European Union, the Nordic Council, the Conference of NATO Parliamentarians, and the Benelux Interparliamentary Consultative Council.

7. *Cultural diplomacy* and informational activities.

8. *Economic diplomacy*—that is, economic activities encompassing aid, loans, investments, and trade agreements.

9. *Diplomacy through technical assistance,* which under favorable con-

ditions might become a genuine people-to-people diplomacy, such as the Peace Corps.

10. The term *military diplomacy* may be used to describe the vital role of defense considerations in national security and the increased role of military officers in diplomatic activities. This is particularly true in NATO, but it also occurs elsewhere. Members of the US Military Assistance Advisory Groups (MAAG) are negotiators, advisors, and inspectors in many countries.

11. *Diplomacy of disarmament and limitations of armaments* form important specialized branches of diplomatic activities for two related reasons: a general desire for peace and the extremely dangerous nature of modern weapons. Since these negotiations cannot eliminate the underlying causes of armaments, they are characterized by long and frustrating discussions during which most negotiating countries would like to appear more peace-loving than the others. Thus the highly technical disarmament negotiations often develop into a make-believe diplomacy, little connected with the realities of international politics.

12. *Intelligence diplomacy*. The confrontation of open societies with the closed system of totalitarian dictatorships has created unequal conditions and has made imperative the increased use of intelligence personnel and intelligence research in diplomacy. A popular myth considers this necessary development a sort of "private eye" diplomacy.

13. Subsidiary arms of diplomacy are *activities of private groups and individuals* in international affairs.

As appears from these categories, functions and methods of diplomacy have not remained unchanged. Some of these methods and forms came from traditional diplomacy, such as bilateral negotiation through diplomatic channels or multilateral negotiations at international conferences. Most are recent developments. Diplomatic methods do not exclude each other; they often overlap and can be used in many combinations. Thus contemporary diplomacy is not unlike an orchestra: a band of performers and a great many instruments. Success of the concert depends on the talent, alertness, and spirit of the conductor. If he gives the right signs, the musicians will play in harmony. But it is easier to satisfy an audience in Carnegie Hall than the heterogeneous multitude in that enormous arena of international politics where nations with varying cultural backgrounds and often conflicting national interests react differently to the same symphony.

The general adoption of the Vienna Conventions on Diplomatic Intercourse and Immunities, worked out by a United Nations conference in

1961, will facilitate international contacts, but lasting success of diplomacy requires a world community with shared moral values in which all nations cooperate and compete primarily in achievements. Such a community is more an aspiration than reality. International life is still similar to a jungle in which reason and good will are not sufficient for survival.

Contemporary democracies have inherited methods and rules of diplomacy developed in a relatively uncomplicated world dominated by a small number of European states. Since foreign affairs are not static, stubborn attachment to tradition and conservatism in method may lead to disaster. In diplomacy a particularly strenuous effort is demanded of the democracies to meet contemporary challenges. How can we preserve world civilization if huge nations are ruled by ruthless despotism? How far can Western diplomacy go in the struggle against totalitarian regimes without jeopardizing the fundamental principles and values of democracy? This is a crucial diplomatic question of our time.

TWO

The Triumph and Decline
of Traditional Diplomacy

The Historical Background

After the breakdown of the hierarchical order of the Middle Ages and the emergence of the national state as a basic unit in international relations, the peace of Europe was secured by the balance of power and traditional diplomacy developed as a necessary corollary of the modern state system. The sovereign national states refused to recognize a superior authority, but at the same time their mutual interests required international contacts through diplomatic representatives.

Although modern diplomacy thus developed as part of the new European state system and consequently dates its major beginnings to the fifteenth and sixteenth centuries, some forms of diplomacy existed throughout recorded history, and its development probably began in intertribal relations. International negotiations would not have been possible without recognition of the immunity of envoys, which is one of the oldest rules of international law. Rules for international conduct existed in ancient China and India as well, but these empires were worlds for themselves and had little contact with the rest of mankind. Consequently, their practices had little influence in other regions.

Developments in Greece and Rome had a more general effect. Some Greek and Roman ideas, formulas, and procedures have influenced international practices throughout the ages. Common worship and a considerable amount of cultural unity developed in the Greek city-states, and some aspects of their system were similar to practices found in modern Europe.

They established politico-religious federations and occasionally submitted conflicts to arbitration. Messengers, orators, and even actors and musicians practiced an early sort of diplomacy in the Greek city-states. Envoys participated in the debates of the assembly of other city-states—the first example of international conferences. The Greeks even developed a kind of consular system which means that permanent consulates preceded by many centuries the establishment of permanent embassies.

While Greek achievements in political philosophy have been unparalleled in history, the Greeks were rather casual in organizational matters and legal formulations. The Romans inherited Greek philosophical ideas and used them as a foundation of their much more effective political, administrative, and legal system. Roman foreign policy relied more on might than diplomacy. The Romans nevertheless contributed substantially to international relations, notably the notion of *bellum justum,* just war. A war to be just required a formal declaration and fulfillment of other ceremonies by special priests, the *fetiales.* During the Middle Ages and in recent decades the material conditions of a just war have become a much-debated topic. Not even the League of Nations or the United Nations could devise generally accepted definitions of "aggression" and "defensive wars." Much depends on interpretation in these fields. Communist leaders consider wars for "national liberation" just wars, probably without knowing that they are using a formula inherited from the Romans.

Another Roman contribution was the idea of *jus gentium,* the law of nations, first developed by the *praetor peregrinus,* a special judge who dealt with cases in which foreigners were involved. In contradiction to the rigid system of *jus civile,* the law of nations took into consideration rules and principles of foreign laws. Later the broadest interpretation of *jus gentium* included elements of international law and even natural law, the common law of all mankind. What was "right" according to natural law was applicable to all nations, and this later implied even a set of vague principles concerning international conduct.

The greatest Roman contribution to international relations was the *Pax Romana,* the organization of a united empire, with an excellent public administration and an expanding system of law. If the expansion of Rome was achieved primarily through military conquest, the universal Roman Empire was based not merely on force but on legal order, good administration, and technological achievements, such as excellent roads and aqueducts. The benefits of a unitary system of law were gradually extended to all peoples within the Empire and the law became territorial for the first time in history under Caracalla in A.D. 212.

After the collapse of the Roman Empire, tribal rules and tribal systems of law replaced the majestic unity of the Roman system and for several centuries made difficult the organic development of international relations in Western Europe. The Roman idea of a universal state survived the destruction of the Empire. Christianity advocated universal ideas, and the idea of universality remained important during the Middle Ages in the *Republica Christiana,* the Christian Republic, based on two institutions, the Church and the Empire. Unlike the old Roman Empire, the medieval Christian Republic had no central organization. It had a common faith, common culture, common language of learning, and similar political institutions based on the hierarchical feudal order, but this was a rather loose setting. On the other hand, the intellectual unity of the Christian states greatly facilitated cooperation and created an atmosphere favorable to the development of rules for international conduct.

The Eastern Roman Empire further developed some aspects of Roman law and the ceremonial functions of diplomacy. Byzantium did not possess the strength of the old Roman Empire and was more influenced by Greek thinking than by Roman. Thus Byzantine diplomacy began to play neighboring states against each other. To practice this refined method of diplomacy, it was necessary to know the domestic problems of foreign states, and reporting on conditions of foreign countries became a regular function of Byzantine diplomacy. Some reports of Byzantine envoys are important sources for historians. In the West, after centuries of turmoil, the Papal Court of Rome and the renaissance city-states in Northern Italy increased and diversified the functions of diplomats. The Holy See maintained systematic international contacts through papal legates and other representatives. Through promulgation of the Peace of God and the Truce of God, the Papacy tried to abolish or at least to restrict private warfare; and these endeavors necessitated diplomatic activities. The Popes acted many times as mediators or arbiters between Christian states. Church Councils formulated certain procedural rules which were later accepted by international conferences as well.

Trade played an important role in the development of diplomacy. This accounts for the prominence of Venice and the German cities associated in the Hanseatic League. In a world of limited travel, merchants had more relations with foreign countries than did most other people.

Developments were most interesting in Northern Italy where the city-states had a marginal position in the general feudal system of Europe and could engage in competition among themselves. They developed practices comparable to those of modern states.[1] In the thirteenth century and later,

---

[1] Mattingly points out that in the early fifteenth century the large West European states lacked the resources necessary to establish stable governments on the national

Venice played a leading role in international politics and codified numerous rules of diplomacy, some of which are still valid. In the second half of the fifteenth century the Italian city-states began to establish permanent diplomatic missions, a practice soon followed throughout Europe. Until that time, ambassadors had been sent on special occasions only, and their missions were of temporary character.

Besides negotiating specific issues, envoys usually reported on domestic conditions. This is the reason why the ambassador became a professional observer as well and was considered in many countries a "public spy." Partly because of this dubious reputation, permanent embassies raised numerous problems. What measures should be taken against an ambassador who conspired against the ruler to whom he was accredited? What kind of immunities and privileges should be extended to the ambassador's family, household, and official retinue? Should the immunity of the embassy include the right to grant asylum to criminals and political refugees? Who should decide precedence in official diplomatic functions and ceremonies? Precedence was an all-important tangle for centuries, particularly after the establishment of permanent embassies. Great international lawyers such as Gentilis, Grotius, Zouche, and Bynkershoek discussed these questions and worked out some general principles concerning diplomatic immunities and privileges. Most problems connected with precedence were not settled until the Congress of Vienna in 1815.

Almost simultaneously with the establishment of permanent diplomatic missions the international scene underwent fundamental transformations. A new weapons system and new means of transportation and communication changed the environment of diplomacy. Permanent armies adopted the general use of guns in the fifteenth century. The full-rigged sailing ship made possible the extension of European empires beyond the seas. The Portuguese, the Spaniards, and later the British, Dutch, and French conquered much of the globe, extending the European balance to other continents. Annexation of territories overseas became known as colonialism.

A revolution in the communication of ideas took place through the printing press. This new method of communication made possible the expansion of Protestant doctrines in many countries, greatly facilitating the spread of ideas. Popular movements began to play an important role throughout Europe. Traditional authorities were challenged, and thousands of people fought against each other in most cruel ways, because of religious and political convictions. While in the preceding centuries the Muslim con-

---

scale. This was possible in the Italian city-states where a relatively wealthy population was concentrated in a small political unit which could easily mobilize its resources. Garrett Mattingly, *Renaissance Diplomacy* (London: Jonathan Cape, Ltd., 1962), p. 59.

quest of Spain and later of the Balkan peninsula restricted the range of European power, the religious wars devastated the central part of the Continent. Nevertheless, a continued growth of the European state system and an organic development of rules for international conduct took place roughly between 1500 and 1914. The discovery of America and the appearance of the balance of power system are important stages of the modern era.

Traditional diplomacy began to function amidst such revolutionary circumstances, in a truly changing world. The age of classical diplomacy was the eighteenth century, when the ambassador in a foreign land was still plenipotentiary in the true sense of the word. His full power to negotiate and conclude agreements was necessary when the stagecoach provided the most rapid means of communication.

Acquisition of overseas colonies was accompanied by the expansion of Western ideas and methods, including diplomatic practices. Until the French Revolution and the Napoleonic wars, a multiple balance prevailed in Europe. Most wars were fought for specific purposes and the multiple balances secured substantial leeway for diplomacy even during the hostilities. Because of the general course of world events, external pressures, and domestic troubles, the power of some European countries gradually decreased and they ceased to be independent states, temporarily or definitively. Venice, Hungary, Bohemia, Portugal, the Netherlands, and Poland are examples of this process. Power-political changes in the various European regions influenced one another; both great and small powers changing allies according to their interests. Separate balances interacted on some occasions. This system made possible many political combinations, flexible policies, and changes in alliances, and thus required frequent diplomatic negotiations.

France became a leading European power, and after Cardinal Richelieu's time French diplomacy was a model in many ways for European states. Richelieu concentrated responsibility for foreign affairs in the Foreign Ministry (1626), and in his famous *Testament Politique* he put forward diplomatic principles of permanent value.[2]

The role of diplomacy thus greatly increased. As the famous French diplomatist Callières, explained in 1716:

[2] For the development of diplomacy and international relations consult: Ragnar Numelin, *The Beginnings of Diplomacy* (New York: Philosophical Library, 1950); Sir Charles Petrie, Bt., *Earlier Diplomatic History, 1492-1713* (London: Hollis and Carter, Ltd., 1949); *The Political Testament of Cardinal Richelieu: The Significant Chapters and Supporting Selections,* translated by Henry Bertram Hill (Madison: University of Wisconsin Press, 1961); Pierre Renouvin, ed., *Histoire des Relations Internationales,* 8 vols. (Paris: Librairie Hachette, 1953-1958); Sir Harold G. Nicolson, *The Evolution of Diplomatic Method* (New York: The Macmillan Company, 1954).

To understand the permanent use of diplomacy and the necessity for continual negotiations, we must think of the states of which Europe is composed as being joined together by all kinds of necessary commerce, in such a way that they may be regarded as members of one Republic and that no considerable change can take place in any one of them without affecting the conditions, or disturbing the peace, of all the others.[3]

Nineteenth-Century Developments

The principles of nationality, self-determination, and other ideas of the French and American Revolutions powerfully influenced politics in Europe during the nineteenth century.[4] These ideas helped in the creation of a united Italy and the German Reich, and gradually undermined the Turkish Empire, Austria-Hungary, and eventually all colonial empires. Still, the rather conservative political system after the Napoleonic wars succeeded in maintaining general peace and order. During this peaceful period the industrial and scientific revolutions began to transform society. The importance of the working class increased together with the mass production of goods. Trade unions and other organizations of workers appeared. State boundaries did not prevent the flow of ideas. Marxism and other socialist ideas became the source of various revolutionary ideologies and social movements in industrialized European countries. The originally liberal ideas of nationalism were often abused by unscrupulous politicians for jingo-nationalistic purposes.

Despite the obsolescence and substantial inner corrosion of traditional European society, these new ideas, movements, and changing conditions of life had little influence on the international political framework as established after the Napoleonic era. The Congress of Vienna had created the foundations of nineteenth-century statesmanship and diplomacy. Napoleon's aggressions brought about the Quadruple Alliance which became an organized cooperation among the victorious great powers, Austria, Great Britain, Prussia, and Russia. With the admittance of France to the Alliance in 1818, the powers cooperated within the political structure of the Congress of Vienna for maintenance of the *status quo*. Congresses and ambassadorial committees of the Alliance functioned as a rudimentary international government from 1815 to 1822. This alignment of leading

[3] Monsieur de Callières, *On the Manner of Negotiating With Princes,* trans. A. F. Whyte (Notre Dame, Indiana: University of Notre Dame Press, 1963), p. 11.

[4] Clausewitz recognized that "the prodigious effects of the French Revolution abroad were evidently brought about much less through new methods and views introduced by the French in the conduct of War than through the changes which it wrought in state-craft and civil administration, in the character of Governments, in the condition of the people, etc." Carl von Clausewitz, *On War,* new and rev. ed. (London: Routledge and Kegan Paul, Ltd., 1949), III, 129.

powers is often called the Holy Alliance. The label is a misnomer, because the Holy Alliance was nothing but a declaration of intent, signed by almost all European powers, to follow Christian principles in their policies.

The major reason for the failure of this post-Napoleonic system was a sharp disagreement on the interpretation of the *status quo*. What Great Britain meant greatly differed from the interpretation of the autocratic continental powers. According to the British conception, the *status quo* was the territorial settlement of 1815 and the exclusion of members of the Napoleonic dynasty from the French throne. The continental states supplemented this idea and intended to maintain the constitutional *status quo* as well. They pledged support for existing political regimes. This meant collective intervention to defend legitimate monarchs in case of popular revolts. Britain rejected the principle of legitimacy and refused to support policies aiming at intervention in the internal affairs of other countries. As the continental powers intervened and suppressed popular revolts, the rift between themselves and Britain widened and the Quintuple Alliance came to an end. Leading European powers considered the possibility of intervention for the re-establishment of the legitimate Spanish ruler in Hispano-America. Britain opposed European intervention in the Americas and the Monroe doctrine made clear the position of the United States toward European intervention in the Western Hemisphere.

Even after the dissolution of the Alliance, the great powers continued to assume responsibility for the settlement of major international controversies, and dealt with problems endangering the peace. The governments of leading European countries established through voluntary consultation a system of informal cooperation, the Concert of Europe, which facilitated settlement of many potentially explosive international issues. The Concert operated through regular diplomatic channels and *ad hoc* conferences, with the Great Powers meeting whenever the international situation seemed to demand action. It was understood in this period that the price of all-out diplomatic victory might be prohibitive, and statesmen were satisfied with the lesser diplomatic objective of accommodation. During the hundred years from the Congress of Vienna to World War I, no protracted general war was fought in Europe. Even the establishment of a united Italy and of the German Reich was possible without general war. Bloody wars outside Europe—such as the American Civil War and wars in the Far East—had only peripheral connection with the European system and hardly belonged to the purview of the Concert of Europe.

The powers of Western and Central Europe usually supported the ramshackle Turkish Empire, the "sick man of Europe," against Russian expansion. Turkish backwardness and particularly the recurring anti-Christian atrocities and massacres in the decaying Ottoman Empire did not facilitate the success of Western diplomacy. In the Crimean War (1854-1856) Great Britain and France supported Turkey against Russia. At the close of the war the Congress of Paris admitted Turkey to the advantages of the public law and the Concert of Europe. The same Congress regulated some important problems of international law, such as the rights and duties of neutral powers in maritime war, and neutralized the Black Sea. During the Franco-Prussian war Russia unilaterally denounced the neutral status of the Black Sea, but the London Conference of 1872 declared that abrogation of treaties must be a collective act of the contracting parties and that the clause *rebus sic stantibus* cannot be invoked unilaterally. The Peace Treaty of San Stefano (1878) between Russia and Turkey was revised by the great powers at the Congress of Berlin (1878) which established a settlement for the Balkans.

During the nineteenth century some technical developments greatly influenced diplomacy. Before the invention of the steamship, the railroad, and the telegraph, the means of overland transportation and communication had remained essentially unchanged for over two thousand years. The Roman Empire had a better road system than did many European states around 1800. With the nineteenth-century revolutions in transportation and communication, the ability of governments to receive information on world events and to send instructions quickly to their diplomatic representatives had a great effect on foreign political decisions, and influenced particularly the relations between envoys and governments. The railroad and steamship, the telegraph and later the telephone facilitated control of the government over diplomatic establishments abroad. In turn, envoys could send information and policy suggestions to their governments more rapidly. The upshot was, as Albert Sorel has pointed out in his remarkable essay on diplomacy and progress, that the new conditions greatly increased the importance of emotion and passion in diplomacy.[5] The chancelleries tried either to eliminate these factors from foreign political decisions or in some cases to use them. Assembling a conference was still difficult. Statesmen had plenty of time to make up their minds as long as a trip from Paris to London took four to five days, from London to Vienna two weeks.

The industrial revolution had an enormous effect on society. Machines and factories made possible ever-increasing production of commodities, and the common man began to realize that he could greatly improve the conditions of his life. This process, coupled with the new communications,

---

[5] Albert Sorel, *Essais d'histoire et de critique,* 3rd ed. (Paris: Librairie Plon, 1913), pp. 271-85.

fundamentally changed many aspects of human relations and had far-reaching effects in domestic and international affairs. Markets and raw materials were necessary for the modern industry that developed first in England, then in Western Europe. Thus during a new era of colonialism, the activities of the Old Continent expanded to world dimensions. The European nations divided substantial parts of the globe among themselves.

Under European leadership progress was taken for granted. European military power and administrative ability made resistance to European expansion impossible. The new colonial imperialism was especially expansive after the 1880s. The solution of conflicts between European powers was facilitated by deals, mutual concessions, and establishment of zones of influence mainly in areas beyond the seas. Large-scale colonialism developed in Asia and Africa without major resistance, and the native regimes were overwhelmed by European power and technique. Industrialization also made substantial progress in two major extra-European countries —the United States and Japan—and by the turn of the century these countries were recognized as great powers with regional interests in world affairs. Great Britain recognized the United States' overwhelming power position in the Americas in the course of the Venezuelan boundary dispute (1895-1897) and concluded an alliance with Japan in 1902.

Simultaneously with this evolution, local and national economies began to develop a world economy. Stock exchanges played an important part in this process. Their activities reflected the economic interdependence of nations. World economic conditions became serious considerations in international politics. Commercial firms vastly increased their operations and called for information and support from consular and diplomatic representatives.

Under the pressure of increased international intercourse and technological development, some modest transfers from national to bilateral and multilateral control occurred, mainly in nonpolitical fields. In Europe the earliest subjects of international regulation were the great rivers crossing or separating several states. For a number of problems bilateral solutions proved to be unsatisfactory, and multilateralism was accepted in a great many fields. International health commissions appeared in some important ports. The foundation of the Red Cross in 1864 was a landmark in humanitarian international organization. The first successful effort toward universalism was in the technical field with the founding of the International Telegraphic Union in 1865 and the Universal Postal Union in 1874. States transferred certain government functions to these agencies, which had permanent secretariats or bureaus. Coordination of national policies in some technical fields was worked out by specialists, whose activities served the common interests of participating states. The first international civil servants, in the inconspicuous garb of specialists, thus appeared on the diplomatic scene. At technical conferences technicians came into contact with each other. They settled questions without the intervention of diplomats.

The cooperative political and intellectual climate of the era facilitated the development of a legal framework in international relations.[6] The Jay Treaty in 1794 had established mixed claims commissions for Britain and the United States, and after the Civil War the Washington Treaty of 1871 and the subsequent Alabama Arbitration gave a powerful impulse to international arbitration not practiced in the seventeenth and eighteenth centuries. The two Hague Peace Conferences developed and formalized methods for peaceful settlement of international disputes, established the Permanent Court of Arbitration, and codified such important segments of international law as the laws of war and neutrality. While the First Hague Conference (1899) was mainly a European affair, with twenty-six participating states, in the Second Hague Conference (1907) forty-four states participated, including many American states.

While the European state system was reaching the peak of its development, the growing body of international law was restricted to the Christian states, and was sometimes called, not without reason, the "public law of Europe." The United States and the Latin American countries, after attaining recognition, automatically became junior members of this community, to which they belonged culturally. When the Ottoman Empire, Japan, and other non-Christian states were admitted to regular membership in this exclusive club, they accepted the principles developed by European states to govern international relations.

Although popular interest in foreign affairs gradually increased in almost all countries, foreign policy decisions were still made by a few experienced statesmen. These men, and the professional diplomats enjoyed similar social and educational backgrounds and shared values across national boundaries. The diplomatic language was not influenced by ideology, and diplomats meant the same things when they used internationally accepted terms. French replaced Latin as the language of diplomacy in the eighteenth century, and the diplomats of some leading countries even wrote reports to their home governments in French.[7] Major participants in world

---

[6] See for details, F. S. L. Lyons, *Internationalism in Europe, 1815-1914* (Leyden, Holland: A. W. Sythoff, 1963).

[7] The peace treaties concluded after World War I introduced the equality of French and English languages and this bilingual rule was followed by the League of Nations as well. The United Nations has five official languages: English, French, Spanish, Russian, and Chinese.

affairs accepted certain unwritten rules of diplomacy. Though the objectives of governments were different and often conflicting, there was tacit agreement on the rules of the game. Promotion of national interests was, of course, the primary purpose of diplomats, but the means and objectives of diplomacy were limited by accepted moral principles and intellectual ideas. Guizot in his *Memoirs* characterized the unity of professional diplomats in the mid-nineteenth century.

> Professional diplomatists constitute in Europe a distinct society, which has its peculiar maxims, lights, manners, and desires, and maintains in the midst of the disagreements or positive conflicts of the states it represents, a tranquil and permanent unity.[8]

Before World War I, all important European states, with the exception of France, Switzerland, and Portugal, were monarchies, and the family ties and personal contacts of the monarchs often supplemented the efforts of diplomats. Continuity and some consistency in European foreign politics was strengthened by monarchs and their advisers. The monarchs may have wanted more territory and power, but they did not want to annihilate their adversaries. This attitude led to moderation and a measure of stability in international relations. However, this personal and functional continuity was not a substitute for wisdom and statesmanship. It could not balance the narrow-mindedness of monarchs and ruling circles and the corrosive effect of new ideas, and it could not prevent the disintegration of ramshackle empires unwilling or unable to carry out internal reforms. Even so, it did facilitate the handling of foreign policy and smoothed international intercourse.

The development of parliamentary democracies and the changing political climate increased the importance of other institutions for securing continuity—the foreign ministries and the diplomatic service. It was realized that, while political leadership and domestic trends may change frequently, foreign policy could not undergo abrupt change or even the appearance of change without prejudice to the national interest. In leading democratic countries the foreign office became the foremost government agency, with an authority above party politics, and the highest foreign service officers were trusted advisers of political leaders.

Developments were different in the United States. Foreign policy was extremely important in the early years of the Republic, and the American nation then was fortunate to have great statesmen and excellent diplomats. Early American representatives abroad were outstanding men. But from

---

[8] F. Guizot, *Memoirs to Illustrate the History of My Time,* trans. J. W. Cole (London: Richard Bentley, 1859), II, 251-52.

the 1830s on they were not followed by diplomats of similar stature. Foreign policy became less important in Washington, and the American politicians and public regarded diplomacy with suspicion. The American government concentrated on domestic problems. Many times it looked upon
international conflicts as cases of law, and handled them on that basis. Protection of American citizens and property abroad was a major concern of
American diplomacy. Legalistic and moralistic considerations often influenced American thinking and actions in international politics. According
to Hans Morgenthau:

> The illusion that a nation can escape, if it wants to, from power politics
> into a realm where action is guided by moral principles rather than by con-
> siderations of power is deeply rooted in the American mind.[9]

Morgenthau distinguishes three periods of American foreign policy: the
realistic, the ideological, and the utopian. Although his thesis was strongly
criticized, some outstanding thinkers in the field of diplomacy shared his
views. George Kennan mentioned the "inevitable association of legalistic
ideas with moralistic ones." [10] He pointed out that the legalistic approach
"ignores in general the international significance of political problems and
the deeper sources of international instability." [11] The debate between the
representatives of the "realist" and "idealist" interpretations of American
foreign policy is a continuous affair.[12]

While the United States remained outside the main stream of world
events, democratic ideas had an important effect on the conduct of foreign
affairs within the national state, and on international relations in general.
European leadership and British world power not only secured prosperity
for the European nations but opened doors in many regions for new ideas
and progress. What Western civilization achieved within a short time was a
unique accomplishment in the history of mankind. Even some of the dark
chapters of the colonial period gradually gave way to happier developments.
In most cases the major motive of colonial expansion was commercial benefit, but colonialism also brought permanent improvement in such fields as
sanitation, public health, and education, and in the spread of technology
and engineering as well as public administration. The scramble for colonies

---

[9] Hans J. Morgenthau, *In Defense of the National Interest* (New York: Alfred A.
Knopf, 1951), p. 13.

[10] *American Diplomacy 1900-1950* (Chicago: University of Chicago Press, 1951) p.
100.

[11] *Ibid.*, p. 99. Kennan further developed these ideas in *Realities of American Foreign Policy* (Princeton: Princeton University Press, 1954) pp. 48-49.

[12] See for a comprehensive presentation, Robert E. Osgood, *Ideals and Self-Interest
in America's Foreign Relations* (Chicago: University of Chicago Press, 1953).

took European power and values all over the globe, opening sources of energy and strength for extra-European developments. European scholars contributed to the growth of national cultures in Asian and African countries.

The century that followed the Congress of Vienna in many ways brought a better life for mankind. *Pax Britannica* ruled the waves. Britain introduced good government in many regions and kept surprisingly small military contingents in various parts of her Empire. In Russia a parliamentary system of government arose in the 1900s, albeit haltingly. In China revolutionary ferment began in 1911 in quest of democracy, freedom, and better life. Germany's political life made progress. A fundamental reorganization of the Austro-Hungarian Empire on a more democratic and federative basis appeared likely although not before the death of Francis Joseph, whose reign lasted until 1916. On the eve of World War I it seemed that individual freedom and democratic forms of government had a good chance of becoming worldwide. The emergence of the United States as a leading world power and the awakening of nations in Asia and Africa were in the offing. Transformation of the worldwide political framework might have taken place in harmony with the general interests of mankind.

After the Congress of Berlin (1878), however, with the gradual formation of the Triple Alliance and Triple Entente, a rigid bipolar balance of power, a "two-power world," appeared in Europe. The opposing European alliance systems did not facilitate the solution of conflicts, but generated further tension that could not be eliminated by diplomatic maneuvers. The failure of traditional diplomacy in 1914 was a major immediate cause of the outbreak of one of the most irrational wars in history, which in turn triggered a series of catastrophic happenings and fundamental transformations in international relations. Sir Edward Grey's prophetic comment— "The lights are going out all over Europe; we shall not see them lit again in our lifetime"—was justified. A century of hope came to an end.

During the great struggle, reason and constructive diplomacy could not prevail. The peace proposals of the Pope were disregarded. Statesmen who advocated an early peace settlement were silenced even in England, and leading politicians became prisoners of their own propaganda. Eventually at the peace settlement of 1919 political emotions played a much larger role than in 1814-1815, and the peace treaties created more problems than they solved. The four-hundred-year-old state system of Europe was disastrously weakened. Irrespective of the untoward consequences of the peace settlement, in which diplomacy took a small part, World War I made apparent the impossibility of drawing a line between domestic and foreign policies on basic issues. It dramatized the shortcomings of Western civilization. It demonstrated to the world the breakdown of solidarity among the European great powers. The sea between Singapore and Vladivostok was dominated by the Japanese navy during World War I, clearly showing the weakening of European, specifically British, power.

One result of these apocalyptic events was a change in the meaning and importance of foreign affairs for the average man all over the world. The individual realized that his own and his family's well-being depended on events in other continents and on his country's policies toward lands far away. This was an important change, because throughout the nineteenth century most men took only rare interest in foreign affairs. Under the monarchies foreign policy was conducted by a small group of persons who had decisive influence in state affairs. It is true that in democratic countries the responsibility for foreign affairs was transferred from the ruler to the prime minister and foreign minister, who were responsible to parliament. But in reality the electorate and the average parliamentarian usually showed little interest in foreign affairs until the experience of World War I. Developments were similar in the United States. The President and his close political advisers resolved issues of foreign policy. In some instances, popular emotions decisively influenced foreign affairs—as in the war against Britain in 1812 or against Spain in 1898. In general, however, the American public did not show much interest. Any given dispute was considered a separate issue and not a part of the world picture.

And so Europe and the United States and, albeit totally unknown to most of them, the peoples of all continents moved inexorably into the new world of the twentieth century that began with the Battle of the Marne in 1914. Diplomacy, which ceased in Europe as a whole, would never be the same again.[13]

The Effect of World War I

In 1914 it seemed likely that the war would be a continuation of diplomacy by other means, according to traditional patterns. In the early stage of hostilities an almost solemn national unity prevailed in the belligerent countries. The populace received news of the outbreak of war with enthusiasm, cursed the enemy, and supported the war efforts. The great con-

---

[13] For the characteristics of traditional diplomacy, see: Jean Jusserand, *The School for Ambassadors and Other Essays* (London: George Allen & Unwin, 1924); Jules M. Cambon, *Le Diplomate* (Paris: Librairie Hachette, 1926); Aubrey L. Kennedy, *Old Diplomacy and New, 1876-1922: From Salisbury to Lloyd-George* (London: J. Murray, 1922); Sir George Young, *Diplomacy Old and New* (London: Swarthmore, 1921); Harold Nicolson, *Diplomacy* (New York: Oxford University Press, 3rd ed., 1963).

flict appeared as a short heroic venture. The German Emperor declared that his soldiers would be home "before the leaves fell." Highly emotional patriotism united the liberals, conservatives, and socialists in belligerent countries. Lenin, then in Switzerland, was greatly disappointed in the Social Democratic parties and was tempted to despair of the revolution breaking out in his lifetime. In this patriotic atmosphere secret diplomacy continued to operate quietly according to the spirit of the nineteenth century, scoring some successes in both belligerent camps. But the political atmosphere changed radically in 1917, and thereafter revolutionary political factors influenced the foreign policy of some of the major contestants. Events had outrun the framework of diplomacy, and statesmanship lost control.

Lenin and President Wilson, in turn, and for different reasons, delivered fatal blows to traditional diplomacy. After the first Russian Revolution in March 1917, the Bolsheviks used popular slogans for domestic and international consumption. Lenin denounced imperialism and promised immediate peace, land, and bread to the Russian people. As a basis for a peace settlement, designed to facilitate revolution, he advocated the principles of no-annexation and self-determination for people in all countries. On the day following the Bolshevik seizure of power on November 7 the new government promulgated a Peace Decree that asked "the immediate opening of negotiations for a just and democratic peace." Lenin and his Commissar for Foreign Affairs, Trotsky, made lavish use of the rostrum of the Soviet government for open diplomacy by propaganda. They addressed their appeals to the peoples of the belligerent nations. To expose tsarist and Western bourgeois regimes, the Soviet government, with utter contempt for diplomatic traditions, published in November and December 1917 the secret treaties concluded by the Allied powers. A Soviet delegation used the subsequent Brest-Litovsk peace negotiations with the Germans as a sounding board to publicize Bolshevik ideas for the general peace settlement.

The fanatic communist minority in Russia unscrupulously drove for power with singleminded purpose and great organizational ability. Lenin's pattern for revolutionary action served its purpose. It was fate's supreme irony that the German General Staff had made possible his return to Russia in hope that he would oppose Russian participation in the war. Lenin certainly did this, and much more. The Communist task was facilitated by proclamation of a program which promised quick remedies to the oppressed, suffering, and maladministered Russian people. Democratic political forces in Russia and abroad only belatedly understood the unprecedented historical situation. Into international relations the communist regime introduced diplomacy by large-scale propaganda and subversion. Soviet proposals for peace were presented with a deceptive clarity and forcefulness. These techniques were applied in the defeated countries with considerable success after the collapse of the Central Powers.

Western statesmen soon recognized the danger inherent in the diplomacy by propaganda of clever and unscrupulous manipulators, and President Wilson gave expression to this general apprehension in his address to a joint session of Congress on December 4, 1917. Wilson was convinced that secret diplomacy was the villain of international politics, and he therefore participated with gusto in the new open diplomacy by lofty proclamations addressed directly to people in foreign countries. Thus, in the last stage of the great struggle, war aims and peace proposals were debated openly, although the secret treaties concluded by the Western Allies in 1915-1916 lingered in the background. Wilson's famous Fourteen Points, set out in his address to Congress of January 8, 1918, effectively countered the Bolshevik peace program. His ideas met with unprecedented success, and in 1918 he was considered the prophet of a new and better world order. As a result of his great influence at the peace table, the idea of the League of Nations was accepted and the Covenant of the League inserted in the peace treaties. But his victory, followed by a political defeat at home, proved pyrrhic on the world scene.

Some of the momentous results of World War I were the temporary eclipse of the two major European countries, Germany and Russia, and the dissolution of Austria-Hungary. The settlement of the Congress of Vienna could not serve as an example at Versailles because the international situation was infinitely more complicated in 1919 than in 1815. Talleyrand had played a major role at the Congress of Vienna, but after World War I the defeated countries were excluded from the peace negotiations. Russia, still torn by a civil war, did not participate in them. The boundaries between Poland and the USSR were established only after a Polish-Russian War by the Peace Treaty of Riga in 1921. The Paris Peace Conference was the first major peace settlement at which the European states were not a majority, and consideration of affairs of other continents naturally meant playing down the importance of European problems. The "Big Four" under President Wilson's leadership sought to replace the balance of power with collective security built around a League of Nations having universal character.

THREE

The League of Nations and Diplomacy in the Inter-War Period

After World War I the League of Nations provided a new theater for international affairs, through the practice of open diplomacy by conference. The conference method was not entirely new. Its modern version had been developing since the seventeenth century. The great European congresses, such as those of Westphalia (1648), Utrecht (1713), and Vienna (1814-15), established international order for long periods, improved conference procedures, and laid down new rules of international intercourse. *Ad hoc* international conferences played an important role throughout the nineteenth century. Their number and scope increased. During World War I, the Allied War Council and diplomacy by conference were important factors in the victory of the Allied Powers.[1]

Practices introduced subsequently by the League of Nations were in harmony with these developments, though they added a few important new features—above all, publicity. The Assembly usually met once a year, the Council more often. Both major organs could deal "with any matter within the sphere of action of the League or affecting the peace of the world." Rules of procedure of the Assembly and Council were similar to independent conferences, but specialists in the League Secretariat improved conference techniques. In addition to periodic meetings, the League sponsored and organized special conferences on a wide variety of subjects, such as financial

[1] Lord Hankey, *Diplomacy by Conference* (New York: G. P. Putnam's Sons, 1946), pp. 10-26.

and economic matters, communications and transit, health, obscene publications, white slave trade, passports, and international relief. This host of nonpolitical conferences demonstrated not only the complexity of modern international problems but also the common interests of mankind. Diplomats remained in the background at these conferences on functional and technical problems. The role of experts grew. Specialists often became negotiators, and control of the foreign ministry over such negotiations weakened sometimes to the vanishing point. The Conference and Governing Body of the International Labor Organization, with its tripartite composition consisting of delegates from governments, employers, and workers, established a new model for multilateral negotiations. The various unions and technical agencies established before 1914 operated independently and had only casual contacts with each other; Article 24 of the Covenant of the League of Nations attempted their centralization.

Politically the most important and novel fact of the interwar era was the presence of many statesmen and diplomats at the Council and Assembly meetings and *ad hoc* conferences sponsored by the League. Attendance of foreign ministers and prime ministers at Geneva ceased to be a sensation and became a regular part of the diplomatic scene. Although in important cases confidential contacts usually preceded and paralleled the open meetings, representatives of many states indeed debated issues of international politics before the eyes of the public. Since transportation and immediate communication were available, politicians could remain absent from their capitals for considerable periods, and they took over functions formerly reserved for diplomats as a matter of course.

The public character of these League meetings was in sharp contrast to the practices of traditional diplomacy. True, with the development of constitutional and democratic regimes, some slight changes in traditional diplomacy had taken place in the decades preceding World War I. The Second Hague Conference in 1907 was the first great international gathering that admitted the public to its plenary meetings. While the Peace Conference in 1919 negotiated and made decisions in closed sessions, at the plenary meeting it too opened the doors to newspapermen.

President Wilson and Lloyd George had discussed the meaning of publicity in connection with negotiations and eventually agreed to a statement on publicity issued at the Council of Ten to the press in January 1919. This statement expressed the basic principle in the following terms:

> The essence of democratic method is not that deliberations of a Government should be conducted in public, but that its conclusions should be sub-

ject to the consideration of a popular Chamber and to free and open discussion on the platform and in the Press.[2]

Most *ad hoc* conferences after World War I followed practices similar to those accepted at The Hague Conference of 1907 and at the Paris Peace Conference. The public was admitted to plenary sessions, though the settlement of politically important questions was prepared in committee meetings or in informal conversations. Wilson's hopes had come true.[3] Geneva in the heyday of the League became a center of open diplomacy by conference. Publicity entered the formerly secret world of diplomacy by the front door at Geneva.

Ever since, public diplomacy has been the subject of heated debate, and perhaps one can conclude that when and whether public discussions are useful in solving delicate international problems depends on the particulars of a case. Admittedly, in most cases it is difficult for governments to make concessions once positions are openly taken. Sounding-board diplomacy often stirs ill-feeling in the interested countries, and creates obstacles for a reasonable settlement by compromise. Prestige plays an important role in international politics, and serious arrangements even in private business are not prepared by statements in the marketplace. Open diplomacy by conference does not always facilitate political bargains or compromise based on mutual concessions. But it is in harmony with the practice of constitutional democracies and satisfies a growing popular interest in foreign affairs.

Surely, for good or ill, this new method became even more meaningful because of the greatly increased role of newspapermen in international life. Press and radio facilitated the focusing of public attention on diplomatic activities. Not only were some functions of diplomats taken over by statesmen and specialists, but management of foreign affairs was closely scrutinized and influenced by the sharp eyes of newspapermen. This was a more

[2] U.S. Department of State, *Papers Relating to the Foreign Relations of the United States, The Paris Peace Conference 1919* (Washington: United States Government Printing Office, 1943), III, 621.

[3] President Wilson proposed in his Point I: "Open Covenants of peace, openly arrived at, after which there shall be no private international understanding of any kind but diplomacy shall proceed always frankly and in the public view." Considering the suggestion that agreements be "openly arrived at," diplomats of Allied Powers were surprised to see that in Paris Wilson himself negotiated behind closed doors guarded by marines.

One of the results of Wilson's proclamation against secret diplomacy was Article 18 of the Covenant, which provided for compulsory registration with, and publication by, the League Secretariat of every treaty entered into by any member of the League. Article 102 of the UN Charter contains similar provisions, although the legal consequences of nonregistration are different in the League and United Nations systems.

striking phenomenon at Geneva than elsewhere, because of the concentration of international activities along the shores of Lake Léman. Diplomacy by conference and the publicity connected with it corresponded to popular trends and opened unprecedented possibilities to versatile newspapermen. In all major countries coverage of foreign affairs became more extensive and far better than before 1914. It was not sufficient for the journalists to listen to speeches. The most important part of their job was interpretation and analysis, for which private contacts and interviews with delegates were necessary. Their work supplemented the functions of diplomats. Foreign ministers sometimes have found better information in reports and editorials of newspapermen than in confidential reports of their own ambassadors. The efficiency and alertness of reporters greatly helped popular interest and knowledge of foreign affairs. International politics left the discreet circle of traditional diplomacy and became the concern of a much wider public.

Publicity in diplomacy often has serious drawbacks. In delicate situations state interests require negotiations through confidential channels, but "leaks" and other unwarranted forms of publicity may defeat this purpose. What is more important in such cases—public knowledge or the success of negotiations? For many newspapermen, publicity is of overwhelming importance although public knowledge is not a substitute for statesmanship. In the early stages of negotiations publicity usually is more harmful than necessary.

Another novelty of world affairs after 1918 was the enhanced role of the small powers. Nineteenth-century diplomatic congresses had paid little attention to the small powers, and a similar practice prevailed at Paris in 1919 when the important problems were discussed by the Supreme Council, the Big Four, or the Big Three. But in the League Council and Assembly the small powers participated in debates on the basis of equality, and their voting and alignment on some occasions influenced the final outcome of diplomacy at Geneva. In the Council the nonpermanent members gradually increased from four to twelve. In the Assembly a canvassing procedure came into being in which the great powers often courted the small states. Assembly sessions provided a public forum for the small powers. Individual brilliance was noted irrespective of the size of the plenipotentiary's country, and some small power representatives had much importance in the League, contributing substantially to the political climate at Geneva. Smaller states usually sent their best known statesmen and diplomats to League sessions, and the influence of some of them was considerably greater than the power positions of their countries would indicate.

Much seemed to have been changed at the shores of Lake Léman; yet the changes were often more apparent than real. The invasion of politicians, experts, and newspapermen at Geneva, the broadening functions of international organizations, and the enhanced role of small powers did not cause essential political changes in world affairs, as long as the international scene was dominated by European powers. In this respect the situation did not change much between the world wars. In fact, one of the internal contradictions of the League system was that between its world aspirations and its overwhelmingly European character. This fact helped foster the illusion that Europe was still the power center of the world. In reality, however, the Great War and the peace treaties had destroyed the European state system, and the League was an inadequate substitute for that system in power politics and its success was limited mainly to social and humanitarian fields.

The important achievements in international politics, such as the treaties concluded at the Washington Conference of 1921-1922, and the Locarno agreements of 1925, were attained outside the League, through traditional diplomacy, as if the League did not exist.

The Washington Conference was a striking example of the effective use of parliamentary diplomacy. In his opening address Secretary Hughes did not restrict himself to the usual diplomatic amenities, but to the great surprise of the other delegations he announced in concrete terms the American plan for naval disarmament. After his speech Hughes adjourned the Conference, "giving the startled delegations three days in which to recover their equilibrium, to study and digest the American plan, and also to feel the worldwide popular repercussions from this extraordinary beginning." [4] The Washington Conference combined disarmament with a political settlement. The Four- and Nine-Power Treaties created a political equilibrium in the Far East which made acceptable the agreement on a limited naval disarmament.

Another ostensible success of American diplomacy was the Kellogg-Briand Pact of 1928, accepted by almost all states although in some cases with important reservations.[5] The contracting parties renounced war "as an instrument of national policy in their relations with one another." But the Pact was not connected with the League and did not establish another organization for carrying out its clauses.

The futility of the Kellogg-Briand Pact and the breakdown of the League system was demonstrated by the Japanese conquest of Manchuria in 1931-

[4] Harold and Margaret Sprout, *Toward a New Order of Sea Power* (Princeton: Princeton University Press, 1940), p. 153.
[5] See Robert H. Ferrell, *Peace in Their Time: The Origins of the Kellogg-Briand Pact* (New Haven: Yale University Press, 1952).

1932. The decisive blow came from Italy in 1935-1936. Mussolini conquered Ethiopia on the pretext that bellicose Ethiopian soldiers "attacked"
Italian troops at Wal Wal on the borders of Italian Somaliland. The League
applied only ineffective sanctions against Italy because Britain and France
did not want to apply measures which could have led to war. Mussolini declared that the extension of sanctions to oil would be regarded as an un-
friendly act—and so oil sanctions were not applied. The fate of Manchuria,
Ethiopia, Austria, and Czechoslovakia clearly showed that the League was
unable to maintain international order when great power interests were involved. For the same reason, the League could not control the international
effects of the Spanish Civil War and did nothing against Hitler's treaty
violations. In the League's declining period Geneva became a fools' paradise.
Democratic governments proceeded in foreign affairs as if nothing had
changed, even while revolutionary transformations were permeating the
fiber and core of world politics. As early as 1932 Winston Churchill had
well characterized the situation when he remarked: "I cannot recall any
time when the gap between the kind of words which statesmen used and
what was actually happening in many countries was so great as it is now."
The greatly increased activity of politicians in the field of diplomacy was not
conducive to the quiet thinking essential to constructive, long-range planning
in foreign affairs. Publicity for publicity's sake, activity for activity's sake,
and quick results to impress fellow citizens were sometimes considered
necessities in democratic countries; but a candid discussion of unpopular
international issues was avoided whenever possible. The growing influence
of an uninformed mass opinion on the conduct of foreign policy increased
the confusion of political leaders who wanted to remain popular with their
electorates. Few advocated rearmament or called attention to the threatening
military might of totalitarian dictatorships and the worldwide activities of
aggressive ideological forces. "Mr. Baldwin's confession, in 1936, that he
did not dare to propose re-armament as he could not 'think of anything
which would have made the loss of the election from my point of view more
certain,' is a good illustration of how democracy can jeopardize the highest interests of the state." [6] While Maxim Litvinov delivered statesmanlike
speeches at Geneva,[7] Nazism and communism fought a bloody war in

[6] Sir Victor Wellesley, *Diplomacy in Fetters* (London: Hutchinson & Co., Ltd.,
1944), p. 124.

[7] "From September 18th, 1934, until a few months before the ontbreak of the Second
World War, Russia continued to be a convinced supporter of the League. Her records
in the Council and the Assembly, and her conduct towards the aggressive powers,
were more consistent with the Covenant than those of any other great power." F. P.
Walters, *A History of the League of Nations* (London: Oxford University Press,
1952), II, 585.

Spain and conducted their cold wars against the democracies by means of fifth columns and large-scale propaganda.

In this self-deceiving political climate, Hitler obtained concessions from the West that the powers had refused the Weimar Republic. This temporizing attitude and the general lack of political determination, coupled with the military weakness of the West, had a devastating effect on men's minds. The principle that might makes right seemed to be accepted in international relations, particularly after the reoccupation of the Rhineland and the seizure of Austria. Shortly afterward, the Munich Conference and the Nazi-Soviet Pact raised the curtain for another act in mankind's twentieth-century tragedy.

During these untoward developments of the interwar era, trained diplomats played secondary roles. More often than not, they were left out of important consultations and negotiations. While in the eighteenth and nineteenth centuries diplomats were employed in international affairs as physicians were in cases of illness, modern dictators preferred party men, and some democratic leaders even were inclined to disregard their experienced diplomatic representatives. It is characteristic that in the 1920s and 1930s the influence of the Foreign Office in Britain declined and the influence of well-meaning but ignorant politicians and publicists increased. Rowse's observations concerning the role of the Warden and some leading members of All Souls are particularly revealing for this process.[8] Events culminated in the pre-Munich period when Chamberlain neglected the Foreign Office altogether. He preferred such amateurs as his special emissary to Hitler, Sir Horace Wilson, who did not tell the unpleasant truth but bolstered the Prime Minister's optimism over getting along with the Nazi leader. It would not be just to blame diplomacy proper for the disastrous events of recent decades. A leading American diplomat, Hugh Gibson, has rightly pointed out that diplomacy "hasn't even been given a chance to fail." He gave strong arguments in support of this thesis. He pointed out that what was called diplomacy in the interwar period has failed to achieve results and has led to disaster. This new method was not really diplomacy. "It was the usurpation of diplomatic functions by politicians and inept amateurs," he said. This meant that politicians, amateurs, and adventurers negotiated complicated world problems in a simplified way—that is, they used unproved, spectacular methods in critical times. Publicity stunts became primary considerations. Political leaders negotiated directly and were inclined to make startling statements instead of pondering the arguments

[8] A. L. Rowse, *Appeasement: A Study in Political Decline, 1933-1939* (New York: W. W. Norton and Co., Inc., 1961).

calmly at home before final decisions. "The result has been a contribution to a world-wide mess of unprecedented proportions." [9]

Hugh Gibson's points are well taken. The Western democracies were fatally weakened by the ineptness and lack of courage of democratic political leaders who took over the function of diplomats. The diplomatic edifice built without solid foundation in 1919 was gradually undermined and eventually collapsed in the late 1930s under the blows of brown, black, and red dictators.

DEVELOPMENTS IN AMERICAN DIPLOMACY

Although the United States never became a member of the League, developments of diplomatic methods at Geneva and in Washington showed some similarities. During the interwar period, nowhere did publicity for foreign affairs become as important as in the United States. One of the objectives Secretary of State Cordell Hull set himself was "to stimulate an informed American public opinion on international events." He began to hold daily press conferences in the Department of State and noted: "No matter what the congestion of my engagements, I had a certain hour set six days a week at which to receive the news and radio correspondents and answer their questions to the best of my ability." [10] Although many of Hull's press conferences were rather uninformative, he established a pattern in the conduct of American foreign policy. But abroad few foreign ministers, if any, followed his example. Most foreign ministries appointed a spokesman and established a division dealing with press and information matters. In the United States even the President and the Secretary of State regularly gave press conferences. [11]

Publicity in foreign affairs was more important and had a different meaning in the United States than elsewhere. Leading columnists acquired probably greater influence in American public life than newspapermen ever had in any other country, with the possible exception of Great Britain in the 1920s and 1930s. Before World War I newspapermen went abroad only for special occasions, but in the 1920s leading American newspapers

[9] Hugh Gibson, *The Road to Foreign Policy* (Garden City, N.Y.: Doubleday and Company, Inc., 1944), p. 63. See for details Gordon A. Craig and Felix Gilbert, eds., *The Diplomats, 1919-1939* (Princeton: Princeton University Press, 1953) and Sir Lewis Namier, *Personalities and Power* (London: Hamish Hamilton, [1955]).

[10] *The Memoirs of Cordell Hull* (New York: The MacMillan Company, 1948), I, 218.

[11] See for the role of public opinion and the press: Lester Markel *et al.*, *Public Opinion and Foreign Policy* (New York: Harper & Row, Publishers, Inc., 1949); Bernard C. Cohen, *The Press and Foreign Policy* (Princeton: Princeton University Press, 1963).

established a network of permanent correspondents in such important centers as Paris, London, Berlin, Moscow, Tokyo, and Geneva.

Perhaps part of the new American interest in foreign affairs came because of the novel American economic position throughout the world. Although the United States never became a member of the League, and although even in 1935 the Roosevelt Administration could not obtain a two-thirds vote in the Senate for ratification of the revised Statute of the Permanent Court of International Justice, isolationist policies could not change the fact that this former debtor nation had become the creditor of the world. Exports increased and became important to some branches of American industry. The new economic and financial posture of the United States caused a marked broadening of American responsibilities abroad. This new situation had an effect on American diplomacy. The foreign investments of American business enterprises multiplied and many American businessmen traveled abroad. These conditions compelled greater consideration of economic factors in American diplomacy and necessitated sending officers with economic training to foreign diplomatic posts. An informed and more interested public and businessmen with interests in foreign countries demanded diplomats of high quality. Reorganization of the American foreign service and unification of the diplomatic and consular services through the Rogers Act in 1924 was a response, though an inadequate one, to the new needs.

In the 1930s several minor reorganizations took place in the Department of State, but the number of officials dealing with foreign affairs showed only slight increase. The total number of positions in the Department of State, American foreign service, and related organizations was 4,726 in 1930, 5,444 in 1940; the figure skyrocketed to 26,449 in 1950.[12] The great increase of officials in the State Department and the Foreign Service reflected the abrupt change of American responsibilities in world affairs. With World War II, the idyllic period of American diplomacy came to an end.[13]

[12] *The Department of State Bulletin,* XXXII (1955), 541.
[13] See for the development of American diplomacy Graham H. Stuart, *American Diplomatic and Consular Practice* (New York: Appleton-Century-Crofts, Inc., 1952); J. Rives Childs, *American Foreign Service* (New York: Henry Holt and Company, 1948); Warren Frederick Ilchman, *Professional Diplomacy in the United States* (Chicago: University of Chicago Press, 1961); Elmer Plischke, *Conduct of American Diplomacy* (Princeton: D. Van Nostrand Company, Inc., 1961); Kenneth W. Thompson, *American Diplomacy and Emergent Patterns* (New York: New York University Press, 1962). See also the various volumes of *The American Secretaries of State and Their Diplomacy,* Vols. I-X ed. Samuel Flagg Bemis, Vols. XI-   ed. Robert. H. Ferrell (New York: Various publishers, 1928-   ); Farag Moussa, *Diplomatie Contemporaine,* Guide Bibliographique, 2d ed. (Centre Européen de la Dotation Carnegie Pour La Paix Internationale, Geneva, 1965).

FOUR

Soviet Diplomacy

Relations with the Soviet Union raised some new problems for which the maxims of traditional diplomacy offered little help. According to Nicolson the activity of Soviet diplomats "in foreign countries or at international conferences is formidable, disturbing, compulsive. . . . But it is not diplomacy: it is something else." [1] While one may agree with Nicolson's preference for the precepts and methods of traditional diplomacy, a negative approach is not useful for dealing with communist governments. Since intercourse with them cannot be avoided and may even increase, the communist states should be recognized for what they are, and handled in the light of their own doctrines and practices.

One of the consequences of communist ideology is the different meaning of diplomacy for the communist and noncommunist countries. The aims and methods of Soviet foreign policy are not difficult to discern. Expansion, subversion and propaganda have always been of high importance. Commissar Leon Trotsky, during the peace negotiations with the Germans in 1918 at Brest-Litovsk extolled the duty of all communists to work for the world revolution of the proletariat, as did the early proclamations of the Soviet regime. Subversion served as a major device of Soviet policy despite a so-called non-propaganda clause inserted in the first commercial treaty concluded in 1921 between the Soviet Government and Great Britain, and despite similar pledges which have appeared monotonously since then both in treaty clauses and public pronouncements. In addition to subversion, the Soviets have preached and practiced the virtues of political flexibility. The periods of cooperation with Germany, 1922-1933 and 1939-1941, like the

---

[1] Harold Nicolson, *The Evolution of Diplomacy* (New York: Collier Books, 1962), p. 121.

era of the popular fronts in the 1930s and the temporary wartime alliance with the Western powers, were only an interlude permitting tactical adjustment in the long-range Soviet political plan. The same is true of Soviet attitudes toward the League of Nations and the United Nations. The policy of Soviet Russia, quite apart from the traditions of Russian imperialism, has a well-defined ultimate objective, the world-embracing Communist state system.[2]

The communists have a central hierarchy and highly organized general patterns and methods to achieve common objectives. There have, of course, been substantial changes and exceptions: Yugoslavia since 1948, Albania since 1960, and, of course, the People's Republic of China. The split between China and the Soviet Union created problems for communist governments and parties in many countries. Their autonomy increased. They have to make a choice between Moscow and Peking, and the various trends of world communism—a new situation for them. The Eastern European countries, in turn, enjoy more leeway in intrabloc politics and even in their relations with noncommunist countries. Although the iron curtain still exists, the days of a centrally directed communist empire are gone. Power struggle within the communist world may facilitate further emancipation of the small communist states. But emancipation has limits because the survival of most communist regimes depends on Soviet support.

Since in a Marxist-Leninist society of states national boundaries would loose their significance, it is difficult to explain the revival of nationalism within the communist camp. Only China and Albania seem to get along with each other in a truly Marxist-Leninist sense. This is understandable in view of the distance and disproportion of power between the two states. Although the Sino-Soviet dispute has been expressed in ideological slogans, in reality it is more a power political conflict which involves territory and spheres of influence. Not much brotherly love exists among the East European communist states either. The increased oppression of the Hungarian minority in Transylvania, for example, has been part of the independent course of Rumanian policy.

It is conceivable that the nature of the problem created by the Soviet Union and other communist states in international politics might be altered by the further deterioration of communist bloc unity and the rise of China in the role of chief "aggressor" state. Even Chinese rigidity is not immutable, and eventually "peaceful coexistence" between Western and com-

---

[2] Elliott R. Goodman, *The Soviet Design for a World State* (New York: Columbia University Press, 1960). For a recent evaluation of Soviet propaganda, see Frederick C. Barghoorn, *Soviet Foreign Propaganda* (Princeton: Princeton University Press, 1964).

munist states might have genuine meaning. But this day is not here yet. Despite disagreements within the communist ranks there have been no fundamental transformations of communist purposes.

Most communist parties are typical fifth columns following the orders of a foreign authority and willing to work against their own states. Moscow and Peking use for their political purposes these extradiplomatic agencies cutting across national boundaries. The general attitudes of the communist parties have proved, particularly between 1919 and 1953, that the foreign policy of the Soviet Government was the policy of communists in most countries, for the communists and fellow travelers closely followed the changes and shifts of Soviet policy. In recent years the Italian and other communist parties have shown some independence, but the strength and meaning of such trends remains to be seen.

Soviet diplomats have broken with the traditions and historical solidarity of the diplomatic profession and have set the clock back several centuries with regard to diplomacy. Soviet views on diplomacy are reminiscent of an age when envoys were considered public spies. Some Soviet diplomats are experts on select problems, particularly well trained in the external forms of diplomacy. They adhere to diplomatic formalities and privileges more than the diplomats of most nations. But the deeper traditions of the diplomatic profession have no meaning for them. Soviet diplomacy is not diplomacy in the traditional sense. The collection and analysis of facts is much developed in the Soviet foreign service, but final evaluation and decision take place in the light of the official party doctrine, which may distort the realities of life. Moscow and Peking judge the outside world according to their own standards, which is one of the reasons why Soviet and Chinese leaders understand little of the strength and weaknesses of free nations.

One can contrast the freedom enjoyed by communist diplomats in noncommunist states with restrictions imposed on Western diplomatic establishments in communist states. Western diplomats live in isolation, their movements restricted. They go to lavish official receptions, but they can have little personal contact with private citizens. Conditions have improved in the USSR and much more so in Yugoslavia and some of the satellite countries since 1956. Yet the basic attitude in most communist states has not changed. Foreign diplomats are particularly isolated in Communist China.

Leitmotivs

Three factors—ideology, power, and personality of the leader—determine or influence importantly the goals and methods of Soviet diplomacy. If communist ideology and the national traditions of Russian foreign policy are probably the most important factors from a long-range point of view, in a concrete situation the power position of the USSR might be more decisive. Power in this sense includes the military, political, and economic power of the Soviet Union, power relations among the communist states, and the prevailing balance of power between the communist and noncommunist worlds. The power positions of the USSR and the United States, NATO and other alliances, interact; and even the USSR's changing power position within the communist orbit tends to influence Soviet diplomacy. Moreover, in a totalitarian government much depends on the person of the dictator and on the character of the power group that surrounds him.

Communist ideology has established a framework for Soviet foreign policy and communist leaders have been quite outspoken about Soviet objectives. The USSR has a dual nature. It is a strong territorial state and at the same time the center and chief supporter of an action-organization based on ideology. Moscow is not only the capital of one of the two superpowers, but the center of a world subversive movement. The historic expansionism of Russia does not contradict communist objectives because territorial acquisitions are partial achievements of the ultimate goal. Although Soviet diplomatic practices have been influenced by Russia's Byzantine and Tatar heritage, the basic world view and ideology of Soviet diplomacy is Lenin's philosophy. Leninism refused to accept an ethical bond between communist and noncommunist states. Lenin's followers feel free to sign and violate any agreements if such actions serve communist interests. Five decades of Soviet foreign policy demonstrate the application of Lenin's advice in international politics, both strategy and tactics. The Soviet Government professes noninterference in domestic affairs of other countries and promulgates a policy of peaceful coexistence; it proclaims self-determination for all people. But in practice this policy is only for special occasions. For example, on March 5, 1960, Khrushchev stated that "the people of Pushtunistan should have the right to determine for themselves through a plebiscite which way they wished to go." He did not make a similar statement during the Hungarian revolution in 1956. The Soviet Government emphasizes the "sovereign independence" of countries in which only the presence of the Soviet Army made possible communist governments.

Agreement on spheres of influence helped cooperation of the great powers before World War I. In August 1939 Stalin made a far-reaching agreement with Hitler on their spheres of influence, and in December 1941 offered a similar arrangement to Great Britain. Khrushchev pointed out several times that Western recognition of existing realities would greatly promote the chances of peaceful coexistence. Such an agreement would include explicit recognition of Soviet domination of Eastern Europe. At the same time, the Soviet Union would feel free to operate through communist parties outside the Iron Curtain and support wars of national liberation. In reality the Soviet Union cannot keep a sphere of influence agreement until it abandons communist ideology as a basis for foreign policy.

We may conclude that communist ideology and the traditions of Russian foreign policy are motives behind Soviet diplomatic moves. They indicate long-range trends in Soviet foreign policy. Although the Soviet government formally participates in the existing international system and enjoys the privileges and advantages of a superpower, in practice communist fifth columns, fellow travelers, stooges, and underground organizations remain tools of Soviet policy. Dissolution of the Comintern and Cominform has not altered this situation.

Besides the ideological factor there is the physical strength of the USSR and the other communist states, a highly important consideration in foreign political decisions. The men in the Kremlin are realistic politicians, inclined to mold doctrine according to the power political situation.

This nonideological factor consists of the military and economic strength of the USSR, the strength and cohesion of the communist states, and the effect of power factors that operate outside the communist orbit. The overall performance and stamina of the noncommunist world is most important.

Military strength and economic power facilitate the operational activities of the diplomacy of any country. After 1957 the greatest advantage of Soviet diplomacy was that the Soviet Union had achieved some spectacular successes in military, economic, and scientific fields. That is why Khrushchev and Soviet diplomats displayed arrogance during this period, with Khrushchev making several contemptuous remarks concerning American strength and performance. Between 1958 and 1962, Soviet leaders repeatedly stated that the balance of world forces had shifted in their favor.

The Soviet attitude has been cooperative on occasion, particularly when external danger along with internal weakness threatened the Soviet Union. It is enough to refer to Maxim Litvinov's attitude at Geneva during the 1930s. After World War II the power political situation changed, and the methods of Soviet diplomacy changed with it. Diplomatic negotiations, particularly conferences with the Soviet Union, presented an amazing picture. The Kremlin often created a crisis by violating an international agreement, by putting forth an unfounded claim, or by supporting an outright aggression or subversion, and then, after much haggling, possibly offered a small concession from its extreme and usually arbitrary position. Stalin's demise did not change these features of Soviet diplomacy. Khrushchev in 1958 created an acute crisis with his speech containing an ultimatum concerning Berlin. When the situation was near explosion, he simply suspended the threat and posed as a peacemaker.

At international conferences Soviet representatives raise procedural issues, repeat arguments endlessly, emphatically deny facts, or connect unrelated problems, and then reverse their position without regard to what they said in previous meetings. Sessions of the Council of Foreign Ministers, the Paris Conference of 1946, negotiations for the Austrian Treaty and for a German peace treaty, the disarmament conferences—all offer examples of such tactics. In the bewildering atmosphere created by this Soviet behavior, even minor concessions on their part bring relief. Diplomatic skill or reasonable arguments are of no avail with Soviet representatives. But once the Soviet Government has decided, in the light of power political considerations, to conclude agreements in specific cases, negotiations go with efficiency and great speed. Final negotiations for the Austrian State Treaty in 1955 are a case in point.

The third factor in Soviet diplomatic behavior—after ideology and military power—is the personality of leaders. Changes in the top leadership since 1953 have demonstrated primarily transformation of procedures and approaches. Despite changes in leadership there has been an essential continuity in Soviet foreign policy. Preparations for some of the policy changes toward the West began during Stalin's closing years.[3] But the rigidity of the Soviet policy that characterized Stalin's postwar rule melted, in the era of his successors, into a diplomacy seasoned with smiles, handshakes, vodka, and outward willingness to cooperate. Stalin's successors even demonstrated by deeds the new era of Soviet policy. They concluded armistice agreements in Korea and Indochina, evacuated eastern Austria and a military base in Finland, and issued conciliatory statements concerning Turkey, Iran, and Yugoslavia. The new Soviet leaders also concentrated on diplomacy by subtle propaganda, almost as if they were applying Dale Carnegie's methods to international relations. Molotov's whistle-stopping tour across the United States, Bulganin's and Khrushchev's many visits abroad, and "smiling Mike" Menshikov's accreditation to the United States are examples. The Bulganin-Khrushchev duo even paid a visit to the communist black sheep, Tito.

Flexible Soviet diplomacy culminated in the 1955 summit meeting at Geneva where both Soviet and American diplomacy seemed to score successes. American and Russian leaders demonstrated to a peace-hungry world that they intended to "coexist," although the word "coexistence"

[3] This is the thesis of Marshall D. Shulman's book, *Stalin's Foreign Policy Reappraised* (Cambridge: Harvard University Press, 1963).

manifestly had different meanings for the two sides. After this meeting American diplomacy relaxed while Soviet diplomacy, in contrast, made full use of the handshakes with American leaders and the friendlier atmosphere created at Geneva.

In contrast to the rigid methods of Stalin, Soviet diplomatic actions under Khrushchev became complex and dynamic. A subtle Soviet diplomacy may serve Soviet interests much more than aggressive attitudes, because conflict-weary Western societies, as well as the uncommitted nations, are inclined to welcome almost any Soviet move that is camouflaged and labeled a "relaxation of tension."

Again, the friendlier behavior of Soviet representatives since 1953 is not entirely new. There were periods under Stalin's rule when the Soviet attitude was cooperative toward the West. Often Stalin personally was able to display great friendliness; at times he could be extremely benign. Ambassador Joseph E. Davies suggested that Stalin's brown eyes were "exeedingly kindly and gentle. A child would like to sit in his lap and a dog would sidle up to him." [4] Major General John R. Deane evaluated him more objectively: "I have seen him fawn over children before the multitude with the same political acumen that prompts similar public displays by American politicans." [5] Cordel Hull thought that "any American having Stalin's personality and approach might well reach high public office" in the United States.[6]

Khrushchev's attack on some of Stalin's abuses at the Twentieth Congress of the Soviet Communist Party in 1956 appealed to the popular imagination, and enhanced the new Russian leader's prestige both in the Soviet Union and abroad. Khrushchev, of course, repudiated only some of Stalin's crimes —particularly the abuses and terroristic methods directed against leading members of the Communist party—but did not criticize Stalin's basic domestic and foreign policies. Khrushchev's speech was not published in the USSR, although many critical comments concerning Stalin have been made public in the Soviet orbit. When this criticism had adverse effects, especially in the satellite countries—since Stalin had been considered the infallible pope of the communist world—there was a cessation of attacks against the dead dictator whose political merits Khrushchev then emphasized.

Still, the new course under Stalin's successors has not been altogether tactical. Although Khrushchev's unorthodox procedures secured him considerable success, the liberalization of Soviet policy that he advocated for tactical reasons escaped control of the communist operators. Mao Tse-

---

[4] Joseph E. Davies, *Mission to Moscow* (New York: Simon and Schuster, 1941), p. 357.

[5] John R. Deane, *The Strange Alliance* (New York: The Viking Press, 1947), p. 291.

[6] Cordell Hull, *Memoirs,* II, 1311.

tung's suggestion of a free expression of opinion within the Chinese Communist party—"let a hundred flowers bloom, let a hundred schools contend" —had similar results. Liberalization was followed by severe repression. Developments in Poland and Hungary, and later Chinese military intervention in Tibet exploded many elements in the communist myth, and thus had an adverse effect on Soviet and Chinese diplomacy. In the case of Hungary in 1956, Soviet difficulties were greatly alleviated by the Anglo-French action at Suez and the subsequent split between the Western powers.

The increasing economic strength and technological successes of the Soviet Union, paralleled by Western inertness, opened a golden age of Soviet diplomacy. The new situation made it possible for Khrushchev to stage his audacious performances before a worldwide audience, and the globe became a theater for this shrewd and jocular fellow. He cleverly advocated peaceful coexistence and cultivated itinerant, and particularly summit, diplomacy. Such friendly exercises alternated with threats and creation of the Berlin crisis in November 1958. Since he was a gregarious person, diplomacy by reception became the order of the day in Moscow, and a great number of leading statesmen went to the Soviet Union. Khrushchev discussed the merits of communism and democracy with Senator Hubert Humphrey in a marathon interview. At the American exhibition in Moscow he provoked a debate with Vice President Nixon before television cameras. Later during his visit in the United States he praised the virtues of communism and peaceful coexistence. He challenged many aspects of the Western democracies during his trip to India, Burma, Indonesia, and Afghanistan. He played the tunes of Franco-Russian amity in France and introduced himself as a great European. After the U-2 incident in 1960, however, he overplayed his hand in Paris and later in the General Assembly of the United Nations. He discovered that diplomacy by shoe-banging did not pay. The failure of his gamble in Cuba was probably a major cause of his downfall.

Khrushchev's visits abroad were most successful when he promised support and gave economic aid. Although some of the statements he made during his visit to Egypt in May 1964 were tactless, huge throngs of enthusiastic, cheering people greeted him everywhere and strengthened the public image of the benevolent, Aswan High Dam-builder potentate. Khrushchev not only promised completion of the second stage of the Aswan Dam within five years, but announced a series of economic grants, and the Soviet Government gave a new long-term loan. Of course, not all of Khrushchev's political journeys were crowned with success. His visit to China did not reverse the deteriorating relations between the two major communist countries. His long-delayed tour of Scandinavia in June-July 1964 was less than successful; official receptions were correct, but the people showed little interest, let alone warm feelings, and his appeals for Denmark and Norway to abandon NATO aroused negative response.

During these propagandistic journeys, Khrushchev pointed out time and again that the Soviet Union was capable of better performance in major fields of human endeavor than were the antiquated capitalistic systems.[7] He illustrated his contention with examples of Soviet achievements in education, industry, science, economics, and military power. Whatever the results, the new method introduced by him in Soviet diplomacy was a real contrast to Stalin's calm and almost introverted attitude. Khrushchev's successors represent new types of Soviet men, that of well trained Soviet bureaucrats and technicians who follow cautiously the traditional lines of Soviet foreign policy. Of course, they seized the advantages offered to Soviet diplomacy by Gaullist France. When Premier Kosygin visited France in December, 1966, he used the occasion for attacks on Germany and suggested that not only military headquarters, but also military alliances should be broken up —a clear allusion to the process initiated by France in NATO.[8]

There is no evidence that Khrushchev's successors are interested in serious talks about Berlin and Germany. The Brezhnev-Kosygin duumvirate seems primarily occupied with domestic and internal bloc problems. But there are major exceptions for which two examples suffice. The one is the substantial military aid to Vietnam. The other is the worldwide support given to anti-United States subversive activities. The First Conference of the Solidarity of Peoples of Asia, Africa, and Latin America, held in Havana in January 1966, was characteristic of the orientation of Soviet activities in international relations. A large Soviet delegation participated in the Havana Conference. About six hundred delegates convened from eighty-two countries. The Conference decided to give increasing support to guerrillas fighting in various Latin American countries, formed a Tricontinental Committee to aid Vietnam, and discussed the liberation of Puerto Rico from "US occupation." This Conference reflected the Soviet support to subversions organized from Cuba in the Western Hemisphere and the training of guerrillas in Cuba for African countries as well. The Soviet and most East European embassies closely cooperate in worldwide subversive activities. In the Soviet apparatus, however, there are apparently at least two distinct tendencies. On the one hand, action-minded communist organizations are bent on justifying their own existence, while at the same time Soviet diplomacy might find a cautious and subtle course more profitable.

[7] See, for his arguments, Nikita S. Khrushchev, "On Peaceful Coexistence," *Foreign Affairs,* XXXVIII, 1 (1959), 6.
[8] See below, Chapter Ten.

As of the spring of 1967 well-organized guerrilla groups have been fighting in Bolivia, Colombia, Venezuela, and Guatemala, and smaller groups have been active in other Latin American countries. Simultaneously with increasing communist guerrilla activities a Soviet trade delegation arrived in Colombia in March 1967, and to the displeasure of Fidel Castro Moscow endeavored to develop commercial and cultural relations with several Latin American countries.

In the shadow of the Chinese convulsion, the war in Vietnam, and the weakening Western solidarity, the Kremlin follows ambivalent policies. Unreliability and unpredictability remain major characteristics of Soviet diplomacy. It is unlikely that trade concessions by Western countries would influence important policy decisions in the Kremlin. Although Brezhnev and Kosygin seem to be level-headed politicians within the limitations of the communist system, they are necessarily influenced by the outcome of a tug-of-war between the hawks and the moderates in the Soviet apparatus. Events may create a showdown situation when the Brezhnev-Kosygin team, separately or together, is forced to make a choice between alternative policies. Since they appear to be realistic politicians, their decision will probably be more influenced by the evaluation of the strengths and weaknesses of the Western nations than by ideological considerations.

DYNAMICS

I turn now to the operational methods, trends, and objectives of Soviet diplomacy. Here one finds a variety of courses. Take, for example, the Soviet policies toward the underdeveloped countries and the uncommitted nations which began in earnest in 1955. The slogan, "who is not with us is against us" was abandoned. In his famous speech to the Twentieth Party Congress in February 1956, Khrushchev recognized a third group of states in addition to the communist nations and the "imperialists." He pointed out that "forces of peace have been considerably augmented by the emergence in the world arena of a group of peace-loving European and Asian states which have proclaimed nonparticipation in blocs as a principle of their foreign policy." Thus a vast "peace zone" embraces "tremendous expanses of the globe, inhabited by nearly 1,500,000,000 people."

Khrushchev's formulation has increased the flexibility of Soviet diplomacy. The USSR appears not only as the fighting leader of the communist camp, but as the eager protector of all nationalist movements that it can use to weaken the Western countries. Although the Soviet Union is not reluctant to apply new methods of colonialism and brutal oppression wherever they seem expedient, Soviet diplomacy supports nationalist movements in the Middle East, Southeast Asia, and Africa, skillfully conducts crusades for peace, campaigns against "imperialists," and deploys its other multi-farious propaganda activities. "National liberation" is seen as the first step toward a communist system. Khrushchev expressed this old communist precept quite bluntly in connection with revolution in Iraq in 1958. "The Arabs are not Marxists," he said. "They are fighting under another flag— under the flag of nationalism. We hail them. National liberation is the first step."

In political maneuvering the most important questions in the world competition between communist and noncommunist states are those that pertain to economic problems of the new nations. The growing industrial might of the Soviet Union has been a crucial factor, and Khrushchev undertook personally to sell Soviet products, technical knowledge, and ideas to the uncommitted millions. Launching of the two sputniks in the autumn of 1957 and the subsequent manned space flights and moon shots have made the Soviet people immensely proud of their country, convinced that they have proved themselves to the world. Under the improved domestic conditions in the USSR, popular enthusiasm for Soviet achievements in the space and missile fields created a favorable atmosphere for bold diplomatic maneuvers.

Khrushchev at the height of his personal power declared his intention to defeat the United States and the other Western countries in production and in conquest of space, believing that the Soviet Union had the industrial capability and technology necessary to achieve this double victory. He loudly proclaimed that the historical process assured communist victory, although whenever possible he tried to give a helping hand to the historical process. Increased Soviet industrial production made possible an effective economic diplomacy on a world scale. This diplomacy included trade agreements, economic and technical aid, and gifts. It leap-frogged into the Middle East, expanded in Asia, Africa, and Latin America. A dispute on fishing rights opened Iceland to economic penetration, even though an important American base was there. Soviet foreign aid was small compared to United States aid, gifts, loans, and investments abroad, but it has been effective in selected strategically located countries, such as Afghanistan or the United Arab Republic. Soviet diplomacy endeavors to establish the image of a rich and powerful USSR that gives unselfish aid to its less fortunate brothers without interfering in their domestic affairs, although, in fact, economic arrangements and agreements on technical assistance might make the recipient underdeveloped countries dependent on the communist bloc. Soviet propaganda seeks to convey the idea that the United States demands a political price for American aid and gifts, while no strings are attached to Sovet economic transactions. In numerous instances aid and technical assistance were given by East European countries. The Kremlin pressured them to participate in such activities.[8] Communist China is using economic diplomacy in a similar way even during periods of serious economic difficulty at home. However, the cases of Indonesia and Ghana have shown that economic aid and technical assistance are not sufficient to win the allegiance of nations.

In addition to economic diplomacy, Soviet space achievements have impressed people around the globe, greatly increasing the prestige of the Soviet Union. The sputniks and luniks are symbols of Soviet leadership in science and technology. Earth satellites and moon shots excite imagination. People in primitive societies connect such achievements with heavenly power, while statesmen are impressed with military implications of Soviet rocketry and the accuracy of missile shots of 8,000 miles into the Pacific Ocean. These successes, and well publicized American failures, had a temporarily adverse effect on the American image in the world. Fortunately, the American astronauts and moon shots considerably improved this image after 1962.[9]

Then there has been Soviet cultural diplomacy. During Stalin's regime an intellectual iron curtain existed between the USSR and the rest of the world. Since his death ideas are flowing more freely between the West and the Soviet Union. Khrushchev was not afraid of limited exchanges of persons and ideas with Western countries. In the shadow of intercontinental missiles and sputniks, he was willing to compete openly and even allowed establishment of an American pavilion for exhibitions in Moscow, in exchange for similar arrangements in New York City.

Cultural agreements concluded with the United States, Britain, France, and other Western countries are modest manifestations of the new cultural diplomacy. Of course, the Kremlin does not welcome true reciprocity in cultural contacts. The Soviet Union supports mainly those cultural exchanges which inflate its prestige or promote specific interests in scientific, technical, and industrial fields. Research possibilities of foreign scholars in

[8] It should be noted that the communists are not ten feet tall in the field of economic aid and assistance; they have outblundered the Western nations in many cases. See Victor Lasky, *The Ugly Russian* (New York: Trident Press, 1965).

[9] It was suggested in 1957-58 that the United States might counterbalance Soviet space and missile boasts with better propaganda. It is not likely that such a procedure would have been useful. Propaganda backfires if not supported by hard facts. The "policy of liberation" announced during the 1952 electoral campaign is a case in point. Khrushchev's diplomacy cleverly used well-timed Soviet space and missile achievements in the battle for men's minds, but Soviet sputniks were real things and not Potemkin villages. American success in space, the atomic submarines, the growing number of Minutemen and other hard missiles re-established American prestige and power position in the world far more effectively than would propaganda.

the USSR are rather limited. In the Soviet Union only reliable communists are allowed to visit foreign countries. Although extended study abroad can become a source of understanding between nations, short visits may have the opposite effect. Brief exposure to foreign environments may only strengthen prejudices. Short contacts might be useful among professional people, such as scientists, artists, and writers, who speak the same language in their own fields and generally understand one another.

Soviet cultural diplomacy is not all that it is represented to be. True intellectual contact between Soviet citizens and the outer world cannot be allowed because such contacts would show that the realities of life do not correspond to the world view of communism. The Soviet citizen is aware of contradictions between party doctrines and the realities of life within the Soviet Union, but it would be fatal to a totalitarian regime for a large number of citizens to have the same experience on a world scale. Western books and newspapers are not generally available in the Soviet Union. Communist mass media of communication indoctrinate all Soviet citizens from cradle to grave, and foreign influence that would interfere with this process is still limited as much as possible.

Advocacy of peace and disarmament constitutes another area where Soviet diplomacy operates successfully upon mankind's desire for peace. Support of various "peace movements" has remained a permanent feature of Soviet diplomacy since Stalin's days. Sweeping disarmament proposals at the United Nations General Assembly were manifest propaganda moves. But genuine progress is impossible in the field of disarmament as long as the Soviet Government is unwilling to accept international control.

BALANCE SHEET

Despite some changes in diplomatic practices, Soviet diplomacy has remained harsh. "Relaxation of tension" aims at disintegration of NATO and other free world alliances, and in general seeks to decrease Western vigilance. Communist coexistence insists on freedom for world expansion of communism, while all noncommunist political elements are as a matter of course liquidated in communist countries. The Janus faces of Soviet diplomacy show themselves in several respects. While Mikoyan and Khrushchev displayed smiling faces and delivered friendly speeches during visits to the United States, in other countries both of them vehemently attacked the source of all "imperialist evils," the United States. The "Geneva spirit" of 1955 and the "spirit of Camp David" of 1959 had little substance and were of short duration indeed. A few decades ago insulting statements by Soviet leaders would have strained diplomatic relations. Since World War II such statements have become usual events, headlines to increase the sale of newspapers. Moreover, such offensive statements often preceded an offer of conciliation. They formed part of the "off again, on again" pattern.

In 1958 Khrushchev created the Berlin crisis with an ultimatum. In 1959-1962 he displayed a defiant attitude in repeated threats to Japan, an insulting letter to Adenauer, renewal of the Berlin threat, and particularly by his unprecedented behavior in Paris following the U-2 incident. The harsh lines and threats of Soviet diplomacy were useful for the Western nations, as the rattling of Soviet rockets and other threats strengthened Western unity in basic policies. Khrushchev merely followed Stalin's example in this respect, so they both may be considered patron saints of NATO. Provocative Soviet moves were incentives for Western cooperation. Internal difficulties of the Western alliance usually increase when the Soviet Union follows a conciliatory policy. NATO's predicament in recent years is a case in point.

Some of the terms of Soviet conciliatory offers are more repulsive than their threats and invectives because the conditions proposed—if words still retain meaning—involve gradual surrender of Western positions without any Soviet concessions. To the Soviet Union peaceful coexistence in Europe means Western surrender in Berlin, which would lead to surrender in Germany, then Western Europe, with the concomitant destruction of NATO, and further communist advances in Asia and Africa. Nonresistance to the Soviet salami-slice tactic would mean loss of Western positions one by one. Soviet proposals for "abolishing the cold war" are almost amusing because the cold war was created by Soviet doctrines and aggressiveness. Lenin set the stage for this "no peace, no war" situation. Soviet proposals for terminating the cold war were aimed at weakening the Western position, the Soviet Union making no concessions at all.

Few events better characterized the continuing realities of Soviet diplomacy than Mikoyan's visit to Cuba in February 1960. He did his best to stimulate anti-American feeling. He emphasized the Soviet Union's leading position in military power and in science, and reminded the Cuban people that the Soviet Union launched the first sputnik and took the first picture of the back side of the moon: "Those who threaten war now know that we have sent a rocket to the moon, and that we can send it with the same precision to any part of the world. But we threaten no one."[10] Such remarks were not necessary for the conclusion of an economic agreement, but Mikoyan was trying in Cuba, much more openly than during his earlier visit to Mexico, to encourage a growth of communist sentiment. His diplomatic exercises were probably preliminary to establishment of a Soviet Truman doctrine at the door of the United States. When United States

[10] *New York Times,* February 8, 1960, sec. 1, p. 1.

relations with Cuba further deteriorated, Khrushchev challenged the Monroe doctrine and promised not only economic but military aid to Fidel Castro.

This Soviet policy culminated in the missile crisis of 1962 which highlighted the fact that lack of reliability and deception are permanent features of Sovet foreign policy. The shock was considerable because Western public opinion, and even governments, time and again are inclined to overlook the importance of propaganda and deception in Soviet diplomacy. One of the shrewdest American ambassadors in Moscow, Walter Bedell Smith, described in his memoirs how the Soviet government violated the most elementary rules of diplomatic confidence in 1948 during the course of bilateral negotiations with the United States. Smith thought that the incident was important because "it taught all of us, the hard way, that the men in the Kremlin had carried over into peace the tactics of breaking confidence, of indulging in practices of deception, falsification and evasion which we had always hitherto associated only with relations between enemy states in time of shooting war." [11]

Various Soviet drives for peace and disarmament have been accompanied by a development of Soviet military might. Of course, it is necessary to distinguish between Soviet propaganda on foreign policy issues and the positions advanced by Soviet representatives at the conference table. Moscow has a way of transmitting its own appreciation of the very real difference. Gromyko's speeches at the United Nations sometimes bear little resemblance to his talks with Secretary Rusk. In the Cuban missile crisis, however, full-fledged deception continued both in Soviet propaganda and official contacts. President Kennedy's strong reaction apparently restored Soviet appreciation of *Realpolitik*. In his report to the Supreme Soviet in December 1962, Khrushchev explained in the usual Soviet Aesopian language that

> it was not in the interests of socialism to permit escalation of the crisis over Cuba into a world thermonuclear war. Such a war is desired by the aggressive imperialist forces, which, in fear of the inevitable historical prospect of capitalism's defeat in peaceful competition with socialism, reason that if we must die, let us die, so to say, with music, even though this music be the explosions of atomic bombs.[12]

Khrushchev spoke in rather moderate terms of the necessity of "normalizing the situation in West Berlin." A month later he told the Sixth Congress

---

[11] Walter Bedell Smith, *My Three Years in Moscow* (Philadelphia: J. B. Lippincott Co., 1950), p. 157.
[12] *The Current Digest of the Soviet Press*, XIV (January 1963), 4.

of the Socialist Unity Party of Germany in East Berlin that erection of the wall in August 1961 was "a historic date in the development of the German Democratic Republic," but he made only some general comments on the German peace treaty. There was no saber rattling. In effect, the two speeches implied that Moscow lacked the power to impose the kind of a settlement which would be a gain to the communist states. In June 1964 Khrushchev gave Ulbricht a Treaty of Friendship, Mutual Assistance, and Cooperation but wrote into it a reservation which kept control of United States, British, and French access to Berlin in Soviet hands.

Despite the many frustrating aspects of Soviet operation in international politics, an overly pessimistic view of Western relations with the Soviet Union would not be proper. A good future for mankind cannot be secured without a minimum of understanding, if not cooperation, between the United States and the USSR. A limited cooperation is not wishful thinking. Since an all-out conflict between the two superpowers would probably destroy both, it is in their interest to avoid such annihilation. Even without a great Russo-American war, the power position of the two countries would greatly diminish in the event of a proliferation of atomic weapons. Atomic disarmament, or at least restriction of atomic weapons, is a common interest of the two superpowers. Both support the conclusion of a treaty to prevent the spread of nuclear weapons.

Common interests can become incentives for cooperation beneficial for all mankind. The West thereby may influence the Soviet area. American influence in Soviet-American relations cannot affect results without United States leadership—that is, leadership in military power, political determination, and constructive ideas for all mankind. Much depends on what American society will achieve. Here imagination, stamina, perseverance, and moral courage are requisites to success.

During the Cuban missile crisis of 1962, both President Kennedy and Premier Khrushchev saw the consequences of an atomic confrontation for the future of their nations. Perhaps this realization prepared a political climate for a *détente*. One of the practical results of the new policies was a limited Nuclear Test-Ban Treaty signed in Moscow in August 1963. This treaty is more of a symbol than a reality, but if followed by further steps, it might begin a new era of *Pax Atomica*. There are other signs of friendlier relations between the United States and the Soviet Union. The United States has sold cereals to the Soviet Union and other communist states, and the Johnson administration has shown a willingness to expand trade with communist countries. Other manifestations of improved United States-Soviet relations include the direct line between Washington and Moscow, conclusion of new cultural exchange agreements, a consular convention, several agreements to explore increased scientific cooperation in fields such as space research and desalination, and agreement to refrain from orbiting nuclear weapons and to limit space activities to peaceful purposes. Further agreements on cooperation and mutual assistance in space are possible.

Only time can test the reliability of the more cooperative Soviet diplomatic posture. In the Antarctic Treaty, signed in December 1959, the Soviet Union agreed for the first time to unrestricted inspection of an area as a guarantee of enforcement of demilitarization, and this treaty has not been violated. The United States and the Soviet Union are apparently willing to conclude a similar agreement concerning the moon and other celestial bodies. The rift with China, the growing restlessness in Eastern Europe, and serious economic difficulties on the home front might give impulse to friendlier Soviet diplomacy toward the West. But none of the agreements with the Soviet Union has settled basic cold war issues. It is possible, if not probable, that conciliatory gestures of Soviet diplomacy still belong to the realm of tactics. In many relations Soviet foreign policy is as anti-American as ever.

Any optimistic speculations should be grounded in experiences with Soviet Communist tactics over a period of five decades. The self-styled collective leadership of the Soviet Union operates today *fortiter in re et suaviter in modo;* it follows Soviet Russian objectives unremittingly, but skillfully and with studied moderation. Although this policy reflects primarily the more subtle approach of Stalin's successors, the Soviet leaders may be yielding partly to overwhelming pressure. Concessions by Moscow may release forces of great significance, and changes made for tactical reasons may escape from the control of the communist operators. It would be a mistake to exclude the possibility of important transformations in the Soviet orbit, but we cannot be optimistic as to the nature or duration of the changes as long as we face in Russia a totalitarian dictatorship which exploits both its own peoples and foreign nations. After his Vienna meeting with Khrushchev, President Kennedy defined eloquently the fundamentally different world views of Soviet and Western leaders.[13]

The Soviet Government has reacted to external factors on many occasions. Changing domestic and world conditions may strengthen sober political trends in the Kremlin. If the Western states remain united and keep their powder dry, Soviet diplomacy might adopt a more cooperative policy.

[13] See below,

FIVE

Summit and Personal Diplomacy

Summit meetings are conferences of leading statesmen—heads of states or of governments—able to make important political decisions and conclude agreements, possibly without consulting ordinary governmental channels. "Summitry" is old wine in a new bottle, for personal meetings of rulers have been well known throughout history. The forms of meetings have changed: the chiefs of Indian tribes smoked peace pipes in America while discussing the terms of agreements.

There are twilight zones between summit meetings and personal diplomacy of leading statesmen. Bismarck and Cavour as well as Disraeli and Churchill each directed the foreign policy of his country and made crucial decisions. They were not reluctant to negotiate directly with foreign statesmen of comparable power. Personal diplomacy was practiced by many kings and emperors. Alexander the Great, Julius Caesar, Charlemagne, Henry VIII of England, Francis I of France, Frederick the Great, and Napoleon Bonaparte negotiated personally with foreign rulers. Such summit meetings sometimes decided the fate of Europe. Napoleon's meeting with Alexander I, Czar of Russia, resulted in the Treaty of Tilsit, an agreement that in some respects was similar to the Nazi-Soviet Pact of August 1939, for the Treaty divided Europe between France and Russia. French and German troops invaded Russia in 1812 and in 1941 respectively, and these invasions led to Napoleon's and Hitler's defeats. Napoleon's defeat was followed by the Congress of Vienna, the first major European summit meeting. Heads of state and other delegates indulged in lavish entertainment while they established a settlement which introduced a new international system and secured general peace in Europe for a hundred years. The system of periodic congresses (1815-1822) gave way to informal cooperation of great powers, called the Concert of Europe. Meetings of statesmen solved international problems and eliminated, at least temporarily, major causes of conflict. Not all such arrangements were made at full summit meetings, but the role of leading personalities was great. The Congresses of Paris (1856) and of Berlin (1878) established a temporary balance between Russia and the rest of Europe, including Turkish provinces in the Balkans. Bismarck and Cavour brought about German and Italian unity, mainly through personal diplomacy and limited wars. In the light of history it is safe to say that personal diplomacy and summit meetings have value as long as the participating rulers and statesmen have the intention and power to conclude agreements and the negotiations are reasonably prepared.

After World War I, the Big Four, Wilson, Clemenceau, Lloyd George, and Orlando, prepared the peace settlement. During the 1920s and early 1930s Geneva was not the only site for gatherings of politicians; leading statesmen approved personally some of the most important political arrangements at conferences outside the framework of the League. The Franco-German rapprochement was initiated by Aristide Briand and Gustav Streseman, who signed the famous Locarno Treaty in 1925. When the impotence of the League of Nations in political matters became obvious, Mussolini proposed the Four-Power Pact, signed by Great Britain, Germany, France, and Italy in 1933. The Pact purported to re-create the old Concert of Europe through cooperation of major representatives of European civilization. Since France and Germany failed to ratify the Treaty, Mussolini's idea was not tested.

On the eve of World War II the diplomacy of dictatorships, with party men in key diplomatic posts, and the growing diplomatc amateurism of the Western democracies, combined to aggravate old problems and create new ones. Mussolini and Hitler met several times and eventually agreed on policies. Meetings between them and meetings between the dictators and Western statesmen were glaring examples of a new diplomacy characterized by lack of preparation through diplomatic channels. Chamberlain disregarded the Foreign Office while he negotiated with Hitler in the Munich era. Events disclosed the lack of reliability, bad faith, and other destructive tendencies of totalitarian diplomacies. Dictators erred often and gravely: Mussolini's diplomatic mistakes precipitated the downfall of Fascist Italy; Hitler's blunders contributed to the destruction of Nazi Germany. The Nazi-Soviet Pact combined with Stalin's overextended faith in Hitler were diplomatic miscalculations. But events likewise disclosed weaknesses of democracies in international politics, for Western foreign policy failed to answer the challenges of a crumbling world order. The prime example of Western diplomatic amateurism was the miscalculation about the intentions of Nazi Germany and Fascist Italy in the 1930s. Later this miscalculation was repeated by the trust and faith that the democratic leaders of the West placed in Soviet leaders.

During World War II, President Roosevelt and Prime Minister Churchill conferred on many occasions, and British and American leaders met with Stalin at Teheran, Yalta, and Potsdam. Their meetings clearly showed the difficulties involved in personal diplomacy by leading statesmen, whenever they have greatly differing backgrounds, different views on the nature of world politics, and mutually exclusive aims and expectations for the future of mankind. Professional diplomats had little part in these negotiations. Even in the West, foreign secretaries under Winston Churchill or Franklin D. Roosevelt did not make major decisions. Roosevelt was his own Secretary of State, in the sense that he made important decisions and on several occasions did not even consult American diplomats.

His chief negotiator in Russian affairs, Harry Hopkins, the head of the Lend-Lease Administration, was a man of exceptional ability but largely ignorant of Russia and communism. Those persons who understood Soviet communism were not even consulted by high policy makers, as the nature of Russian-American relations should have required. The briefing papers for the Yalta Conference were sober and realistic; but there is no evidence that these were studied, let alone appreciated, by President Roosevelt. Sumner Welles has pointed out that President Roosevelt harbored a "deep-rooted prejudice against the members of the American Foreign Service and against the permanent officials of the Department of State." [1] On several important occasions the President acted alone or in cooperation with amiable amateurs without looking into the briefs of specialists and without consulting experts. Neither during the Cairo Conference with Chiang Kai-shek nor later at Yalta did Roosevelt have at his side a political adviser on Far Eastern affairs. Such nonchalant practices at summit conferences and the neglect of elementary rules of traditional diplomacy did not contribute to the West's effectiveness.

President Roosevelt considered the leader of the tottering British Empire as a representative of nineteenth-century colonial imperialism and Stalin as a potential partner in a great human enterprise. At the same time, in Stalin's eyes both Churchill and Roosevelt were the exponents of a doomed capitalist world order. In Roosevelt's mind, the ideological, po-

[1] Sumner Welles *Seven Decisions that Shaped History* (New York: Harper & Row, Publishers, Inc., 1951), p. 216.

litical, and social differences between communism and the Western state system were overshadowed by the immediate military goals and by the rosy future promised by the fraternal cooperation of the Four Policemen. At the Yalta Conference, "freedom," "democracy," "a friendly government," "free elections," meant something essentially different to Stalin and to the English and American statesmen. This is probably the reason why Stalin signed without hesitation the "Declaration on Liberated Europe," which pledged "the earliest possible establishment through free elections of governments responsive to the will of the people."

Under Truman and Eisenhower the role of Secretary of State increased. Dean Acheson and John Foster Dulles enjoyed great political authority and could negotiate and make political decisions in wide areas. Of course, according to the American Constitution, the Secretary of State is the President's agent. His powers are determined by the President. Although in parliamentary democracies all members of the cabinet are responsible to parliament, Foreign Ministers' power depends largely on their relations with Prime Ministers. Heads of government usually have confidence in their own political talent and negotiating skill, and are inclined to indulge in various forms of personal and summit diplomacy. But conferences of leading statesmen are not guarantees of success. Even councils of allied statesmen can easily become sources of misunderstanding. The former Secretary General of NATO, Dirk U. Stikker, noted that he was privileged to see the telegrams emanating from both sides after a high level allied meeting, and commented:

> Both telegrams dealt with the same subjects—the same conversations, in fact—and they were in complete contradiction to each other. Even among the ruling few, the great "men of responsibility," there is a good deal of wishful thinking to the effect that the other side has fully grasped the full implications of some carefully phrased innuendo or intentionally vague expression. When such a delicate point in these talks has been passed, luckily without creating trouble, one will prefer to forget it, while the other will underline it heavily.[2]

Some of the postwar leaders, particularly Adenauer, de Gaulle, Macmillan, Eisenhower, Kennedy, and of course Khrushchev, practiced personal diplomacy. Adenauer did not like summit meetings unless a meeting of minds was in sight, and General de Gaulle was also extremely cautious in this respect. He was only following Phillipe de Commynes' (1471-1551) advice:

[2] Dirk U. Stikker, *Men of Responsibility* (New York: Harper & Row, Publishers, Inc., 1965), p. 369.

Two Great Princes who wish to establish good personal relations should never meet each other face to face but ought to communicate through good and wise ambassadors.

De Gaulle was not reluctant to indulge in a brand of diplomatic tourism. He visited many countries and used these trips to promote his favorite political objectives. His visit to the Soviet Union in June 1966 is an example. The visit was spectacular and proved to be a great personal success. He was the first Western head of state who was allowed to visit major cities in the Soviet Union and address the Soviet people directly through television. He behaved with great dignity and the imponderable results of his public performances may be considerable. This visit was prepared most carefully. France's well-timed separation from her fourteen NATO partners created for him a favorable diplomatic position in Moscow. Despite these advantageous circumstances, talks between de Gaulle and the Soviet leaders resulted mainly in agreements on general principles. A promising concrete result was the agreement for cooperation between the Soviet Union and France in space and science. De Gaulle and the Soviet leaders agreed that the approach to a European settlement should first occur among Europeans. The Soviet negotiators did not contradict the suggestion that United States acceptance of the final agreement was essential, but neither did they show interest in the settlement of major political problems, such as the German question.

De Gaulle's precursors in touristic diplomacy were the dynamic Khrushchev and President Eisenhower during his last two years in office. Both men tried to sell their political ideas in many countries, but the tangible gains of this practice are doubtful. There are special difficulties in the United States, as Dean Rusk appropriately noted:

> It is respect for the Presidency which leads one to believe that visits to 20 or more countries in the course of a few months, interspersed by periods of preparation and rest, take too much out of the man and his office. A presidential system cannot easily adjust to an interregnum; a nation moving with such great mass and velocity needs the engineer at the throttle.[3]

Secretary Dulles disliked summit meetings, having acquired experience in this field during the Paris Peace Conference in 1919 where he witnessed the shortcomings of presidental diplomacy.[4] Despite distaste for the summit,

---

[3] Dean Rusk, "The President," *Foreign Affairs*, XXXVIII, No. 3 (1960), 369. See for detailed information on personal diplomacy of the President of the United States, Elmer Plischke, *Summit Diplomacy* (College Park: University of Maryland, 1958).

[4] Andrew H. Berding, *Dulles on Diplomacy* (Princeton: D. Van Nostrand Company, Inc., 1965), pp. 20-25.

Dulles liked and practiced the traveling technique of diplomacy. In an interview with Martin Agronsky on the NBC television program, "Look Here," he explained in 1957 why he did so much flying.

> Well, I fly because I go to meet heads of government, foreign ministers of other countries, and in a few minutes or at most a few hours of personal consultation you can achieve a much better understanding than you can possibly achieve by going through the processes of communicating through notes and writing to each other.[5]

Debacles in foreign affairs may come from wrong diplomatic methods as well as from shortsighted policies, and often from an interaction of both. Fumbling in policies may involve wrong diplomatic procedure, such as summit meetings before the establishment of a basis of possible agreement through diplomatic channels. Statesmen then face unproductive alternatives. They may have to choose between avowal of failure, acceptance of meaningless declarations, or imprudent concessions. A variation of the latter is the conclusion of ambiguous agreements which the contracting parties later can interpret differently. Often solemn agreements in principle disguise disagreements in practice. Under these conditions, agreements and high-level declarations may become time bombs in international politics, because the same issues arise again and usually under worse conditions. The Teheran (1943), Yalta and Potsdam agreements (1945), the Geneva summit meeting 1955, and the Camp David talks in 1959 are cases in point. The spirit of Geneva in 1955 had little realistic foundation, which was proved by the failure of subsequent meetings of the foreign ministers. The spirit of Camp David was of even less happy memory.

In the 1950s and particularly in the period following the Suez fiasco and the Hungarian revolution, summit meetings were considered valuable for lessening tension between the Soviet Union and the West. The chief advocates of these summit meetings were the British Prime Ministers, Sir Winston Churchill,[6] Sir Anthony Eden, and Harold Macmillan. The most vigorous representative of this school of thought was Macmillan. His arguments for summitry were pragmatic. The school of thought to which he belonged claimed that negotiation with the Soviet Union was unique in

---

[5] As quoted by Dana Adams Schmidt in "Instant Diplomacy and the New Diplomats," *Columbia University Forum,* II (Fall 1958), 36.

[6] According to D. C. Watt, Churchill first called for a "parley at the summit" in his election speech of February 15, 1950. See "Summitry Reconsidered," *International Relations,* II (1963), 493. Watt suggests that talks about a "Western summit" or "Asian summit" misuse the term because a true "summit" must be a multilateral meeting "of the heads of government of mutually opposed inimical countries." *Ibid.,* pp. 496-97. The actual use of the term "summit" is broader than this definition indicates.

that only one Soviet leader, the man on the top, has power to decide. Macmillan's supposition was that Khrushchev in carrying out his manifest wish for a *détente,* might consent at summit meetings to measures he would not entrust to a subordinate. This is the main reason why Macmillan went to Moscow in February 1959. Although he was exposed to abuses and humiliations, he took them with grace and continued to advocate meetings of Western and communist political leaders.

In the United States there was less interest in high-level negotiations with Soviet leaders and it is one of the ironies of fate that the invitation to Khrushchev to visit the United States in the summer of 1959 was extended by Under Secretary of State Robert Murphy as the result of a "misinterpretation" of President Eisenhower's intentions.[7] Khrushchev visited the United States in September 1959 and talked over some delicate issues with Eisenhower at Camp David. Subsequently, the U-2 incident of 1960 affected the atmosphere between the United States and the Soviet Union. Despite worsening relations, Eisenhower was willing to participate in a summit meeting in Paris in May 1960, because he was afraid the armament race might lead to an explosion. He saw no alternative to a summit meeting because diplomacy through ambassadors and foreign ministers proved ineffective. The U-2 incident provided Khrushchev with a pretext for blowing up the conference. He probably had gone to Paris with the intent of sabotaging the meeting and thereby strengthening his position in Sino-Soviet relations. Even before the U-2 incident he realized he could not obtain Western concessions on the Berlin question or any other substantive issue. The meeting gave occasion to humiliate the President of the United States. But Khrushchev's attitude served a positive purpose for the West. It demonstrated that some optimistic assumptions underlying summit meetings were wrong.

The Paris meeting proved once more that summit meetings cannot solve complex political problems. Such meetings serve primarily the purposes of the Soviet Union, provide Soviet representatives with a propaganda forum, and put Western leaders under pressure to yield. Although Khrushchev

[7] President Eisenhower explained in an interview given to the *New York Times* that his idea was to pass along a hint to Khrushchev that if the foreign ministers' conference made progress perhaps there could be an exchange of visits between him and President Eisenhower. But Murphy did not attach such a condition when he extended the invitation in a conversation with Frol R. Kozlov, First Deputy Premier. Khrushchev accepted the invitation and President Eisenhower had to allow the visit even though the foreign ministers' conference did not make progress. The President said in the interview "I think it was my fault" in not making the intention clear. *New York Times,* September 12, 1965, sec. 1, p. 30. Cf. Dwight D. Eisenhower, *The White House Years: Waging Peace 1956-1961* (Garden City, N.Y.: Doubleday and Company, 1965), pp. 405-8.

wrecked the Paris Conference and abused President Eisenhower, the chief casualty of this meeting was the idea of summitry.

After the failure of the Paris Conference, authoritative sources stated in London that Macmillan had not the "slightest intention" of resuming the initiative through another visit to Khrushchev in Moscow. Macmillan told the House of Commons (May 23, 1960) that the lesson of the summit conference was that the West should press forward with the conferences proceeding at Geneva, especially the one on nuclear tests which was progressing not too badly, and later with the disarmament conference. He alluded to the ten-power disarmament conference due to reassemble at Geneva in June 1960. He considered that conference a forum where the West might continue the dialogue with the Soviet Union.

Almost simultaneously with these happenings, Dean Rusk in his article on the American President superbly appraised American-Soviet summit meetings:

> Picture two men sitting down together to talk about matters affecting the very survival of the systems they represent, each in position to unleash unbelievably destructive power. Note that the one is impulsive in manner, supremely confident as only a closed mind can be, tempted to play for dramatic effect, motivated by forces only partially perceived by the other, possibly subject to high blood pressure; the other deeply committed to principles for which his adversary has only contempt, weighted down by a sense of responsibility for the hundreds of millions who have freely given him their confidence and whose fates are largely in his hands, a man limited by conscience and policy in his choice of tactics and argument, a man with a quick temper and a weak heart. Is it wise to gamble so heavily; are not these two men who should be kept apart until others have found a sure meeting ground of accommodation between them? Is there not much to be said for institutionalizing their relationship? [8]

Summit meetings reduce the importance of regular diplomacy and may diminish the authority of nonparticipating states. Participants usually consult and inform their major allies. Consultation took place in the NATO Council before summit meetings with the Russians in 1955. President Eisenhower consulted his allies before receiving Khrushchev in Washington in 1959. After the meeting Khrushchev hurried from Washington to Peking with a short stopover in Moscow. Although he did not bother to consult or inform the East European countries, explanations to Peking were apparently in order.

Some summit meetings have concentrated on the clarification of positions

[8] Dean Rusk, "The President," p. 365.

and the definition of areas of agreements and disagreements. An example of such meetings was the encounter between President Kennedy and Khrushchev in June 1961. In his report to the nation about the "very sober two days" in Vienna, Kennedy said: "No major decision was either planned or taken. No spectacular progress was either achieved or pretended. . . . Our views contrasted sharply, but at least we knew better at the end where we both stood." [9] He clearly defined the major causes of difficulties of negotiation with Soviet leaders:

> The facts of the matter are that the Soviets and ourselves give wholly different meanings to the same words: war, peace, democracy and popular will. We have wholly different views of right and wrong, of what is an internal affair and what is aggression. And above all, we have wholly different concepts of where the world is and where it is going. . . . We believe in a system of national freedom and independence. He [Khrushchev] believes in an expanding and dynamic concept of world communism. [10]

The Vienna conference facilitated the establishment of a neutralist regime in Laos, although the Russians probably would have accepted the same temporary solution in any case. In most other respects the meeting was characterized by controlled clashes between Kennedy and Khrushchev. [11] Conflict between them was particularly sharp about Berlin. Khrushchev's threatening attitude made a deep impression on Kennedy. The harsh atmosphere of the Vienna confrontation was a sobering experience for both of them. Although a personal correspondence was continued and other contacts were maintained between them, they never met again.

One of the important results of the Vienna summit was President Kennedy's decision to strengthen the military forces of the United States. In order to show his determination to resist communist encroachments, he had sent military contingents to Berlin and Vietnam. Khrushchev, in turn, became less enthusiastic about summit negotiations. In reply to an appeal from participants of the Belgrade conference of nonaligned nations, he wired the following statement:

> It goes without saying that negotiations on mature international problems are needed and we have said so on more than one occasion. But they are needed not for the negotiations' sake. Bitter experience has taught us to speak about this straight. Talks would be useful only if statesmen go to these talks with a serious desire and readiness to achieve agreements which

[9] *New York Times,* June 7, 1961, sec. 1, p. 16.
[10] *Ibid.*
[11] See for details, Theodore C. Sorenson, *Kennedy* (New York: Harper & Row, Publishers, Inc., 1965), pp. 541-58; Arthur M. Schlesinger, Jr., *A Thousand Days* (Boston: Houghton Mifflin Company, 1965), pp. 358-74.

would represent a basis for strengthening peace. The participants in the talks must have courage to face realities and clearly realize that no one can turn the tide of events which reflect the national development of human society.[12]

Soviet-American relations since World War II demonstrate no magic formula for solution of differences between superpowers. Basic political problems cannot be solved by personal meetings, smiles, and handshakes. Without careful preparation summit conferences do not lead to good results. Meaningless communiqués are palliatives but not cures. Even the Soviet bloc "summit" meetings are seldom productive. In the West it is often assumed that Soviet bloc conferences involve prior agreements on goals, principles, and methods. This was true in Stalin's hey-day, but in the post-Stalin era such meetings are sometimes meaningless or they reveal unexpected setbacks.

Despite many unfortunate precedents, summit conferences are here to stay because to remain on "speaking terms" is an important objective of diplomacy in the atomic age. Installation of a "hot line" between Washington and Moscow is a symbol of this need. In our time the peace of the world, if not the future of mankind, depends on the superpowers. Although it would be an illusion to believe that contacts and negotiations between Washington and Moscow constitute an automatic guarantee of peace, it is important that political leaders of the two countries have a clear idea about each other's policy in fundamental questions and explore all avenues which may lead toward a more secure world. Dean Rusk, shortly after the publication of his rather critical appraisal of summitry, became Secretary of State and in this capacity accompanied President Kennedy to summit meetings and diligently practiced the traveling technique of diplomacy. Sir Anthony Eden as Foreign Secretary opposed a summit meeting in early 1955. As soon as he became Prime Minister in April 1955 he advocated a "summit." [13] Proposals for summit meetings are, of course, popular in a peace-hungry world, particularly before elections. People are inclined to believe that the "great men" of the world will see the light and agree on peace if they come together. The examples of Dean Rusk and Sir Anthony Eden illustrate that summit meetings and personal diplomacy—despite

[12] *New York Times,* September 23, 1961, sec. 1, p. 4.

[13] See for details, D. C. Watt, *loc. cit.* p. 495. It should be noted that the Soviet Union made a few real concessions, one of which was the signature of the Austrian State Treaty on May 15, 1955. This means that Prime Minister Eden was probably influenced by foreign political and electoral considerations when he supported the plan of an East-West "summit" meeting.

many pitfalls—have become almost unavoidable consequences of contemporary international politics. If summitry and personal diplomacy of leading statesmen are here to stay, their disadvantages can be avoided and their advantages can be maximized by thoughtful preparation through regular diplomatic channels and carefully selected special emissaries.

SIX

The System
of the United Nations

A Changing Pattern

The great political difference between the League of Nations and the United Nations is difficult to overemphasize. It originates not so much in the different legal structure of the Covenant and the Charter as it does in the changed world setting and practices of the two organizations. In the pre-1914 era, relations between the great powers in Europe decided the major issues in international politics, and as a rule the rest of the world was not consulted. Largely because of the absence of the United States from the League, this situation did not essentially change in the period between the World Wars. The extra-European countries did not have an important role at Geneva. When the Soviet Union joined the League in 1934, Maxim Litvinov did not represent a voice of dissent. He appeared as an apostle of collective security and cooperated with the Western democracies most of the time.

The League's Assembly and Council had equal powers and their decisions required unanimous votes in nonprocedural matters. But the votes of states involved in a dispute were discounted in that particular case. In the United Nations the General Assembly and the Security Council have different powers. The Security Council has primary responsibility for the maintenance of international peace and security. Its decisions, mandatory for all member states, must include "the concurring votes of the permanent members." Decisions of the General Assembly on important questions are made by a two-thirds majority of the members present and voting. The Assembly of the League met once a year for a few weeks and the Council met "from time to time" as occasion demanded. The Security Council is a continuously functioning organ and the regular session of the General Assembly lasts several months each year. It is a practice to accept almost any request for placing a situation or dispute on the agenda of the General Assembly. A vast number of subjects are discussed there without preparation through diplomatic channels. The United Nations deals with staggering problems of an ideologically divided world. Its Assembly is a microcosm of the global political situation with all its complications. Principles and standards of international conduct developed by the European states are no longer universally recognized.

While the Covenant of the League was part of the peace treaties concluded after World War I, the San Francisco Conference met during the last stage of World War II, after which there was no general peace settlement. The Charter of the United Nations, signed by fifty-one original member states, was far from perfect; but it probably contained the maximum consensus possible in 1945 between the Soviet Union and the democratic nations, and between large powers and small. The ink had hardly dried on the Charter when it became clear that agreement on principles meant different things for the contracting parties. Wartime objectives of the great coalition were achieved with defeat of the enemy, but the Allied powers were unable to agree on a general peace. The undefined *status quo*—particularly in Germany—aggravated misunderstandings among the former Allies.

The United States endeavored to continue cooperation with the Soviet Union, but the objectives connected with cooperation were defeated. Having renewed the drive for imposition of their political and economic system on the rest of the world, the communists began to use United Nations organs primarily for this policy. Vyshinsky and his successors considered the United Nations a forum for communist propaganda, paralyzed important activities, and supported movements which weakened Western influence.[1] Because of this militant attitude, and excessive Soviet use of the veto, legal remedies for violation of international obligations and the creation of a world security system through the United Nations proved impossible. The United States and other noncommunist nations established their own regional security system on the basis of Article 51 of the Charter. Inserted at insistence of the Latin-American states, this article authorized individual or collective self-defense "until the Security Council has taken measures necessary to maintain international peace and security." In line with Article 51 and a changed American attitude in world affairs, the

---

[1] Alexander Dallin, *The Soviet Union at the United Nations* (New York: Praeger, 1962). John G. Stoessinger, *The United Nations and the Superpowers* (New York: Random House, 1965).

Truman Doctrine and the Vandenberg Resolution heralded a new era in American foreign policy by extending American responsibility for the defense of wide areas.

The worsening relations between the superpowers affected the functions and the balance between major organs of the United Nations. The authority of the Security Council diminished not only with proliferation of regional organizations (NATO, OAS, SEATO, ANZUS, CENTO, numerous bilateral treaties, and treaties within the communist bloc) but even more with the growing importance of the General Assembly and the Secretary General. Although the "founding fathers" had not planned these developments, the broad provisions of the Charter established their legal basis. The United Nations showed great flexibility amidst many unforeseen difficulties. The ineffectiveness of the Security Council made it necessary that the General Assembly or, in some instances, the Secretary General, should act. In view of this situation the General Assembly became, from time to time, the center of United Nations diplomacy where the alertness and mobility of politicians was necessary, in addition to the skill of diplomats. The "Uniting for Peace" resolution of November 2, 1950, recognized and made legal a shift in the structure of the world body, and made possible transfer of cases from the Security Council to an emergency session of the General Assembly to be called on twenty-four hour notice upon vote of any seven members of the Security Council when a deadlock prevented the Council from exercising its primary responsibility for international peace and security. The same resolution authorized the General Assembly to recommend collective measures, including the use of armed forces.

These developments and rapid world revolutionary transformations influenced the powers and activities of the Security Council, General Assembly, Secretary General, and interrelations of these three organs. The United Nations developed into a different organization from that planned at Moscow, Teheran, Dumbarton Oaks, Yalta, and San Francisco.

Simultaneous with these transformations, a great increase in membership has altered the balance in the Assembly between representatives of the major land masses and cultures. Among the fifty-one original member states there were only four from Africa and nine from Asia. During the first decade of the United Nations the growth in membership was slow and the Western nations easily could form the two-thirds majority necessary for Assembly decisions on important questions. The influence of the United States was considerable in most Latin American and Western European countries, and it was not difficult to obtain support for United States policies in the Assembly.

From 1946 to 1954 only nine countries were admitted to the world organization. In December 1955 a package deal between the United States and the Soviet Union allowed sixteen countries to enter the United Nations. Subsequently, the process of admission has accelerated. By 1966 membership had increased to 122, among them thirty-eight African states which constitute the largest regional group in the Assembly.[2] New states are admitted as members almost as a matter of course—in some cases with cavalier disregard for reasonable criteria of statehood and for Article 4 of the Charter which provides for admission of "peace-loving states which . . . are able and willing" to carry out membership obligations. It would have been wiser to admit some new states through a gradual process. During a period of transition, on the basis of Article 81 of the Charter, the United Nations could have helped establish their public administration, train their armies, develop their economies. Such cautious procedure would have facilitated the avoidance of Congo-like situations, and would have served the long-range interests of the new states better than immediate recognition and "no-questions-asked" admission to the United Nations. With the exception of Switzerland, Communist China, and the divided countries, all states are now members of the United Nations. Indonesia left the world organization in 1965 and returned in 1966.

In the early 1960s the majority of new nations have considered many issues on their merits, and have supported collective United Nations interests in some fundamental questions with political maturity. In 1961 lack of support was in large measure responsible for Soviet withdrawal of the famous "troika"[3] proposal, a Soviet plan which would have introduced the veto into executive functions of the Secretary General. The latter could not have acted without the consent of his deputies from the West, communist bloc, and neutral countries. In harmony with the Charter, the international character of the Secretary General and his staff was maintained, and U Thant was elected unopposed—with no "troika"—to succeed Dag Hammarskjöld. In December 1966 he was unanimously reelected.

Many important changes in the United Nations are all the more remarkable because the Charter has not been substantially revised or reviewed by a General Conference, as provided in Article 109. Since amendments to the Charter require ratification by two-thirds of the members, including all permanent members of the Security Council (Article 108), lack of consensus among the permanent members has made important revisions of the

[2] This group ostracized the Republic of South Africa, one of the original member states.

[3] See below, p. 73.

Charter impossible. The only exceptions are the two amendments, approved by the General Assembly in December 1963, which increased membership in the Security Council from eleven to fifteen, and in the Economic and Social Council from eighteen to twenty-seven. These amendments took effect in 1965.

The central figure in the system of the United Nations is the Secretary General, whose powers are unprecedented in the history of international organizations. Unlike the League's Secretary General, he is not only the chief administrative official of the organization but also has political authority. He represents the interests of the totality of the member states much more than any other individual. He administers, coordinates, and may initiate political actions. He can act independently, and can use his office for mediation. The Charter gives him broad powers: he "may bring to the attention of the Security Council any matter which in his opinion may threaten the maintenance of international peace and security" (Article 99). His office combines the functions of an international civil servant with the duties of an international statesman. His initiatives are important. Whenever the Charter or a resolution—frequently couched in ambiguous terms—authorizes the Secretary General to act, one phase or another of his actions may antagonize power groups in the world organization. His unique position cannot be fully effective without the support of opposing power blocs and the majority of nonaligned states—an almost impossible task.

Because of this intricate situation, the limitations placed on the Secretary General, in many instances, are more important than his powers. Although the three individuals who have held this high position have acted differently in order to face specific problems, there has been a continuity of development under them.

Trygve Lie (1946-1953) took some bold initiatives and was probably carried away more easily by his emotions than his successors. Under him there were only two serious crises: Palestine and Korea. He was under attack in the United States and blackballed by the Soviet Union.[4] After him Dag Hammarskjöld (1953-1961), an extremely cautious person, was elected. He did not plan to develop systematically the power of his office, but he responded courageously to new challenges. Although he remained a prudent man, he had to implement vague resolutions which involved decision-making and actions. He was confronted with five major crises: Suez, Hungary, Lebanon, Jordan, and the Congo. He began to assume the role of a world executive in early 1956 with a mediation in Cairo. Later

[4] Trygve Lie, *In the Cause of Peace* (New York: The Macmillan Company, 1954).

during the Suez crisis, he had to negotiate with Nasser because the United Nations Emergency Force could not have entered Egypt without the consent of the Egyptian government. Thus, by the force of circumstances, he gradually secured some special powers for the Secretary General. This became even a greater necessity in the Congo affair. His fatal trip was necessary because the Katangese secessionist leader Tshombe was unwilling to negotiate with anybody else. Both Lie and Hammarskjöld tried to serve the international community and interpreted the Charter according to their conscience in Korea and the Congo. Hammarskjöld in his own inscrutable way was a dedicated champion of a world unborn. His tragic end was a symbol in the contemporary drama. He tried to serve the collective interests of a divided world community—a task similar to the squaring of a circle.[5]

Hammarskjöld's successor, U Thant (1961-   ), as a citizen of a neutralist Asian country, has enjoyed a strong position *vis-à-vis* the Asian and African nations, the Soviet Union, and other communist states. Despite these advantages, he could not solve the conflict which originated in a dispute about the meaning of peacekeeping operations. His underlying problems concerned some basic articles of the Charter and policies of the major powers, and, particularly, the exercise of some collective authority by the world organization. Since the United Nations could not change the power realities of an ideologically divided world, it was unable to settle important political disputes and proved ineffective in the field of peaceful change. Still, in cases of acute conflicts it has been an elementary obligation for the United Nations to maintain or restore peace. This duty is the origin of peacekeeping operations, for which there are no provisions in the Charter.

Antagonism between the permanent members prevented the creation of armed forces under Articles 43-49, for the purpose of maintaining international peace and security. For the same reason mandatory powers of the Security Council have not been tested. Yet in spite of its lack of an army, the United Nations has intervened with some success in several highly explosive situations. Collective United Nations military action launched in Korea in June 1950 was possible because the Soviet Union had boycotted sessions of the Security Council. Even in this case the Council, not using its mandatory powers under Chapter VII, only recommended that members participate in the collective action against the aggressor. Return of the

[5] Wilder Foote, ed., *Dag Hammarskjöld Servant of Peace* (New York: Harper & Row, Publishers, Inc.). Dag Hammarskjöld, *Markings,* trans. Leif Sjoberg & W. H. Auden (New York: Alfred A. Knopf, 1964). Stephen M. Schwebel, *The Secretary-General of the United Nations: His Powers and Practice* (Cambridge: Harvard University Press, 1952). Sydney D. Bailey, *The Secretariat of the United Nations,* rev. ed. (New York: Praeger, 1964).

Soviet representative made the Council powerless, and further recommendations in the Korean war came from the General Assembly.

In the absence of a United Nations Army, small units of the armed forces of the member states have taken part in peacekeeping operations. As early as 1947 the Special Committee on the Balkans used military officers from several member states as observers. In the Kashmir conflict of 1948, the Security Council set up a small observer group of military officers, a group which still existed at the outbreak of hostilities between India and Pakistan in August 1965. The truce between Israel and the Arab states was supervised by approximately 700 United Nations military observers, under the authority of a Truce Supervision Organization which, with some change, is still operating.

During the Suez crisis of 1956, United Nations peacekeeping activities developed further. With the consent of the Egyptian Government, the General Assembly established the United Nations Emergency Force in the Middle East—an army of more than 5,000 men which occupied the Gaza Strip and part of the Sinai Desert and which controlled access to the Gulf of Aqaba. These forces created zones of stability and made possible peaceful work on both sides of the border in these dangerous areas. In the midst of the Lebanese crisis in 1958, the Security Council set up a three-man observer board and authorized the Secretary General to organize an observer group of some 600 officers. The situation changed for the better a few months later, and the observers left. Transfer of New Guinea from Dutch sovereignty to Indonesia in 1963 came after an intermediate period of United Nations administration and occupation by a United Nations Security Force. In 1963 the Security Council approved peacekeeping operations in Yemen, in 1964 in Cyprus, in 1965 in Kashmir and Santo Domingo.

All these truce supervisory and military observer operations dwindle in face of the engagement in the Congo; at maximum strength, about 20,000 soldiers from twenty-three countries participated in it. The United Nations forces were invited by the Congolese Government and the Security Council's resolution of July 14, 1960, authorized the Secretary General to take the necessary steps to provide the Congolese Government with such military and technical assistance as might be necessary until the Congolese national security forces could fully meet their responsibilities.

In the Congo—as elsewhere—contingents sent by small powers acceptable to the local sovereign participated in peacekeeping,[6] although several phases of United Nations military maneuvers in the Congo received logistic

---

[6] In Cyprus British contingents were included in the United Nations force.

aid from the United States. In these military operations the Secretary General had to act as a quasi commander-in-chief—a function unforeseen by the framers of the Charter.

Costs of the two major peacekeeping operations in the Middle East and the Congo created a serious United Nations politico-financial crisis. Costs of minor peacekeeping operations were covered by the regular budget as "unforeseen and extraordinary expenses," but special assessments were necessary in the case of the United Nations Emergency Force in the Middle East and the United Nations Force in the Congo. The Soviet Union, France, and some other states refused to recognize the right of the General Assembly to levy assessments for these operations, but there was an important difference between the position of the Soviet Union and France. The Soviet Government maintained that only the Security Council had the right to send United Nations military forces for peacekeeping; consequently, the actions of the General Assembly in this field were illegal. France challenged the binding character of assessments levied by the General Assembly for peacekeeping operations. According to the French position peacekeeping operations have a voluntary character unless approved by the Security Council. France maintains that, under the Charter, the General Assembly can only make recommendations, and it is the responsibility of states that vote for them to find a solution to financial problems created by their decision. In harmony with this view, France paid her share for the United Nations Emergency Force in the Middle East, but refused to pay for Congo operations or for servicing the bond issue floated to relieve the organization's finances.

An overwhelming majority of states in the General Assembly considered the expenses of peacekeeping operations legitimate expenses of the Organization within the meaning of Article 17, par. 2 of the Charter ("The expenses of the Organization shall be borne by the Members as apportioned by the General Assembly."). This interpretation was strengthened by an advisory opinion of the International Court of Justice on July 20, 1962, which considered the peacekeeping assessments levied by the General Assembly for operations in the Congo and in the Middle East mandatory for all members. Although the Court's opinion on United Nations peacekeeping expenses was accepted by the General Assembly in December 1962, France and the Soviet Union have maintained their position.

Debates about peacekeeping operations and costs affected the basic ideas of the United Nations—in particular, the distribution of functions between the General Assembly and Security Council. Can political resolutions of the Assembly obligate all member states, including those who oppose them? One can argue that financial contributions may involve participation in a policy against which the permanent members could use their veto in the Security Council. If so, the General Assembly would take over some important functions of the Security Council; France claimed it would assume powers of a world government.

Before the 19th Session of the General Assembly, the United States served notice in a memorandum submitted to the Secretary General in October 1964 that it would insist on the application of Article 19, which takes away the right of voting in the General Assembly from any member whose payments are in arrears for the preceding two full years. Article 19 has never been applied, since members—sometimes at the last minute— have paid enough, at any rate, to prevent its application. The Soviet Union became liable to the two-year rule in 1964, because of its refusal to pay the assessments for the Congo and Middle Eastern forces, and the Soviet satellites, France, and other states could have lost rights to vote in the Assembly in 1965. However, the Soviet Union insisted that Article 19 was not automatic but subject to the two-thirds majority rule. The Soviet delegation indicated that it would walk out of the United Nations if Article 19 were applied against the USSR. Eventually, a showdown was avoided at the 19th Session with the adoption of a complicated procedure under which no votes were taken in the Assembly. The absolutely necessary business was settled through private negotiations outside the sessions and a few backdoor ballotings. The purpose of this awkward procedure was the avoidance of a United States-Soviet confrontation. The 19th Session of the General Assembly was appropriately called the "lost session" because very little substantial business was done and some of the meetings produced incidents which would have been more fitting to a vaudeville or operetta scenario.[7] American diplomacy probably committed a tactical error by not following up with the emphatic announcement of the United States intention of challenging the Soviet vote on the opening day of the session of the General Assembly in 1964. At that time the United States reportedly had the necessary majority in the Assembly. As the challenge was delayed, the support slipped away and in 1965 the United States no longer had sufficient backing.

The transformation of the diplomatic climate in the United Nations made necessary the abandonment of a well established position for which American diplomacy fought for several years. Ambassador Arthur J. Goldberg in his maiden speech on August 16, 1965, told the United Nations Committee on Peacekeeping that Washington accepted regretfully the "simple and inescapable" fact of life that the Assembly was not disposed to

---

[7] See for details, Hernane Tavares de Sá, *The Play Within the Play: The Inside Story of the U.N.* (New York: Alfred A. Knopf, 1966).

apply the loss-of-vote sanction of Article 19 against the Soviet Union, France, and eleven other nations that have refused to pay for peacekeeping operations.

The changed attitude of American diplomacy implies that in the future all peacekeeping operations sponsored by the General Assembly will have to be paid either by the participating countries or on the basis of a special agreement—a position advocated by France during the controversy. The new situation will strengthen the position of the Security Council but will preclude certain courses which were possible in the past. The comeback of the Council is perhaps not entirely undesired by American diplomacy in view of a drastically changed situation in the General Assembly. In the past most peacekeeping operations were in harmony with United States policies. But would the United States financially and politically support United Nations operations which would violate American national interests?

Parliamentary Diplomacy

Procedures, debates, use of committees—the entire setting of the General Assembly and other United Nations organs show much similarity to national parliaments. Many rules of parliamentary procedure apply to the United Nations General Assembly and similar international bodies.[8] Even parliamentary tactics can be used and abused there. The similarity is restricted, of course, to appearances, tactics, procedures, and formalities, for the basic purpose and character of national parliaments and United Nations organs are fundamentally different. The one has citizens of the same state, the other representatives of political entities with greatly differing populations, powers, as well as stages of industrial development and civilization. While members of national parliaments make up their minds how to vote, and vote in their own names, delegates in the United Nations follow instructions of governments on distant shores and cast votes in the name of the countries they represent. It is another question how far the delegates of authoritarian states represent interests and public opinion of their countrymen. Many times, national prestige is more important than the merits of a case. While the primary function of national parliaments is to make binding decisions in the form of legislation, the General Assembly is mainly for discussion and has power only to make recommendations—although in

[8] The meaning of "parliamentary diplomacy" was well defined by Dean Rusk "Parliamentary Diplomacy—Debate vs. Negotiation," *World Affairs Interpreter,* XXVI (Summer, 1955), 121-22. For further reference see, Philip C. Jessup, "Parliamentary Diplomacy," *Recueil des Cours,* Tome 89 (Leyden, Holland: A. W. Sijthoff, 1957), pp. 185-320. Kenneth W. Thompson, *American Diplomacy and Emergent Patterns* (New York: New York University Press, 1962) pp. 202-15.

some limited fields, such as internal organization and budgetary matters, the recommendations have binding force. The effect of a political recommendation depends primarily on support of the major powers. As the dispute on contribution to peacekeeping forces has shown, budgetary and political matters can be inextricably interwoven.

Public discussion in the United Nations can be a mixed blessing. To "stand up and be counted" may be heroic, but it is not necessarily good diplomacy. The United Nations offers many possibilities for a troublemaker who can create public issues from problems which could be solved only after preparation through confidential diplomatic negotiation. On occasion, the need of governments to take an open stand complicates the process of constructive solution.

The growth of the political importance of the General Assembly has had several consequences. The fact that the traditional unanimity of diplomatic conferences gave way to a two-thirds majority in the Assembly, combined with equality of voting power of each member state—be it Honduras or the United States—has created a strange situation. States representing only a fraction of the world's population and contributing less than 6 per cent of the budget of the United Nations could dominate the Assembly through the magic two-thirds majority. However, the likelihood of such a minority victory is not great, for most small states depend on some great power for support. Blocks and groups influence policies. One consequence of parliamentarianism in the United Nations is that delegations of member states form blocs according to their world view, traditions, national background, and special interests in the various regions of the globe. But with the exception of the communist bloc, group voting in the United Nations is more similar to a quadrille than a goosestep. Members of the same bloc may take different positions depending on issues. Much depends on American and Western European leadership.[9]

The Afro-Asian states vote together mainly in opposition to everything

---

[9] At present, the Afro-Asian states form the largest bloc; but they are subdivided into numerous groups, such as the Arab League and the Organization of African Unity, with some overlapping memberships. Several Asian states are associated with the Western defense system. The Latin American states form a more homogeneous group with a long habit of cooperation. There are outside the iron curtain seventeen European states in the UN which are members of several regional international organizations. The five Nordic states form a group with special interests of their own. With the possible exception of the Latin American states, membership in all noncommunist blocs is complicated by overlapping regional organizations. The British Commonwealth of Nations is one of the typical overlapping organizations with members in four continents. Cf. Thomas Hovet, *Bloc Politics in the United Nations* (Cambridge: Harvard University Press, 1960) and *Africa in the United Nations* (Evanston, Ill.: Northwestern University Press, 1963).

which smacks of colonialism, a highly emotional issue. This is one reason why Soviet diplomacy endeavors to connect all issues with colonialism and imperialism. In harmony with this policy, Khrushchev's famous address at the 15th session of the General Assembly on September 23, 1960, combined three major topics. He proposed (1) a treaty on "General and Complete Disarmament;" (2) the reorganization of the executive power in the United Nations on the basis of tripartite representation, the so-called "troika" of the Western Powers, the socialist states, and the neutralist states; and (3) a declaration on granting independence to colonial countries and peoples.

The Assembly accepted an Afro-Asian proposal (Resolution Number 1514 [XV]) on the ending of colonialism, which ushered a new era in the United Nations and became for many Afro-Asian nations as important as the Charter itself. The vote was 89-0 with nine abstentions, including the United States. The issue of colonialism, combined with the increasing number of African states, had its own momentum, and in the 1960s dominated many debates in the United Nations. In 1961 the General Assembly adopted a resolution for the establishment of a special committee to expedite the implementation of Resolution 1514 (XV). However, the Assembly did not accept a Soviet proposal which would have set a short deadline for the liquidation of colonialism. The activity of this special committee has become a dynamo of anticolonial drives, with South Africa, Portugal, and Southern Rhodesia as the major targets. This committee has replaced the Committee on Information from Non-Self-Governing Territories, and has assumed other far-reaching powers as well. The dismissal by the International Court of Justice of the case of South West Africa on a preliminary ground in August 1966 poured oil on the anticolonialist fire.

Some United Nations meetings have shown the often topsy-turvey character of international forums. Representatives of an aggressive totalitarian state have been able to ride the anticolonialist waves and to preach in all seriousness about human rights, freedom, and self-determination. The brutal treatment and, in some cases, the liquidation of several religious and national minorities in the Soviet Union—such as the Crimean Tatars, and Turks, the Kalmyks, peoples of the North Caucasus, the Volga Germans, and many others—hardly qualify Soviet delegates for the role of anticolonialist grail knights. While the Afro-Asian nations concentrate on anticolonialism, many prefer to notice as little as possible the dictatorial regimes installed and maintained by the Soviet Union in Europe. A few intelligent leaders of the new states know that colonialism is dead as a political force, but many other leaders continue to use it as a slogan. Under the umbrella of anticolonialism, Indonesia launched an expansionist policy;

India occupied Goa, notwithstanding many Indian statements against the aggressive use of force. Such actions were not seriously challenged in the United Nations. The fundamental question concerns the meaning of freedom. Can the United Nations accept a double standard in self-determination? Is racial segregation worse than oppression of human freedom in totalitarian countries? Is segregation and oppression of colored people by other colored people permitted? Are dictatorial regimes more tolerable in new countries than elsewhere?

Many delegates have expressed their outrage at the anguish of the enslaved, notably and justly with respect to the African victims of South Africa's policies. But the same delegates are inclined to disregard tyranny elsewhere. Colonialism and the flexible notion of neocolonialism have been scapegoats for unrelated developments. This is neither fair nor, in the longer run, realistic. Some political extravagance and opportunism of the new nations can be explained and overlooked. Most leaders have been popular heroes who courageously fought colonialism and almost instinctively continue this battle, though political conditions have changed. The future of the new nations will depend much less on speedy conclusion of decolonization than on solution of domestic problems, particularly the increase of agricultural production and modernization of societies. Economic and other internal difficulties are staggering, and may inspire ill-advised actions in foreign affairs. Asian and African nations are in a hurry to enter the twentieth century and enjoy the industrial age. Western policy should support their efforts in any reasonable way. Still, the nonaligned nations should preserve a sense of proportion and objectivity. Racial discrimination is evil, colonialism outdated. The tide of history is against both; they will disappear and Western nations should expedite this process. But there are many other evil things in the contemporary world, such as aggressive and subversive totalitarian dictatorships, the new imperialism of some of the former colonies, and discrimination based on race, caste, class, sex, and creed. The nonaligned nations should recognize these evils as well, and constitute a bulwark of moral strength in defeating tyranny everywhere.

Small powers have only remote interest in numerous issues debated by the General Assembly. Many small-power delegates do not even have satisfactory information, let alone instruction, for most disputes and problems in the United Nations. Sometimes geographical location and political alignment of a country determine its political attitude. Of course, small powers may trade support and votes for favors. In the United Nations, alignment comes about through informal consultation in group meetings, cocktail parties, and other social gatherings. Small power delegates may play an important role and great powers, in courting the weak and small countries, sometimes modify their positions. A vote-getting campaign in the General Assembly of the United Nations is considerably greater than in the Assembly of the League, where such activity was more limited. One may wonder whether it is a sound policy that the great powers regularly seek the support of small powers. Does this topsy-turvy relation create illusion? All in all, the vote getting procedure, if overdone, is a questionable practice. Small states may exaggerate their own importance and may propose actions beyond their abilities. It is easy to express wishes when one does not have the capacity and intent to contribute toward fulfillment. Lack of power, in practice, may mean irresponsibility. Small power representatives may even make threatening statements without much consequence, while similar statements from a great power representative may cause tension. Sometimes, however, even great powers choose to satisfy smaller friends with rude statements addressed to the latters' enemies. Such actions may have propaganda value. In delicate cases a reasonable compromise solution might be more acceptable when presented by a small state not committed in the issue.

There is a great difference between categories of small states. Some states have a long history and foreign-political tradition. Consequently in their foreign policy the United Nations is only one instrument of diplomacy. But many of the small states which have appeared on the political scene recently lack diplomatic traditions; they rely on the United Nations and can be tremendously influenced through United Nations channels. The United Nations is particularly important to the new states. It provides a school for them not only in international affairs but for the democratic process in general. The General Assembly is a place to engage in parliamentary tactics; it teaches the parliamentary ropes in the rough-and-tumble of world politics. The structure and operational methods of the United Nations correspond to the ideas of Western democracies. While democratic representatives feel at home in the atmosphere of the United Nations, communists have a great handicap—freedom of speech. People talk back and may call the bluff of the official party line—an unusual situation for communists. Most new states have only limited ability to establish embassies abroad, but in New York their permanent mission accredited to the United Nations may have contacts with representatives of practically all states, except the Asian communist countries and East Germany.

The United Nations has introduced some elements of orderly process into the maze of political changes. While the communists advocate revolutionary transformation, Western interests require a slower pace and a measure of stability. Communists usually support the greatest possible acceleration of changes—in many cases the direction of change is immaterial to them—because rapid changes lead to upheaval, revolution, and chaos, which in turn, can be dominated by trained communist organizers. Evolution is less dramatic and less appealing to popular imagination than spectacular revolutions. In connection with emotional issues moderation and reason have little influence. Voting in the General Assembly may become the prize example of political power without responsibility if a combination of small states loses a sense of proportion, develops an exaggerated idea of their own importance, and believes anything goes which is accepted by the Assembly. The 20th and 21st General Assemblies showed abuses of majority voting, including violation of the Charter requirement for a two-third vote on important questions. If abuses continue, reform of the voting system will have to be considered. But a reform of United Nations procedures for rationalization of meetings and reduction of the plethora of speeches is more urgent.

The United Nations will have to solve technical operational problems, such as the increasing meetings of the General Assembly and its committees. From mid-September usually to late December the seven Assembly committees are in almost permanent session. Most questions are discussed in a committee and in the General Assembly. The original procedure was probably satisfactory for the 51 states, but not for a world body, the membership of which has more than doubled and become much more heterogeneous in the process. United Nations membership is a prestige and status symbol for new nations. Many speeches are for home consumption, and some representatives are prone to indulge in verbose addresses—apparently a kind of self-assertion. The torrent of inconsequential speeches, and the ensuing general boredom, may bury constructive ideas. Most delegates want to participate in the discussion of questions of any importance. Debate on a general question usually precedes debate on the specific resolution, and delegates may comment on points of order at any time. Each speech is reproduced in three languages: English, French, and Spanish; final resolutions and documents are also reproduced in Russian and Chinese. Tons of printed papers do not facilitate the solution of difficult problems.

Resolutions of the General Assembly may not amount to much more than pious declarations of intent. In many cases it is impossible to ascertain the effect of a United Nations resolution on an international situation. There are clear exceptions. The composition of voters supporting the resolution is of great importance. In the case of cooperation between the two superpowers, any resolution will become policy. If one superpower manifests strong opposition, a resolution of the Assembly, even if accepted by a massive majority, is wholly ineffective within the sphere of influence of the opposing superpower. Suez and Hungary in 1956 serve as dramatic illustrations of these two alternatives. However, some important Uni Nations actions have taken place against the opposition of the Soviet Union. Establishment of the Expanded Program of Technical Assistance, the Special Fund, and the World Food Program, and continuation of the Congo operation are cases in point. In many instances there is no showdown between the superpowers, and the case apparently can be settled, as far as the United Nations is concerned, through a resolution. Once accepted, resolutions become factors in international politics, and their effect depends to some extent on diplomats and international officials. The chief weapons in Hammarskjöld's successful Middle Eastern negotiations were United Nations resolutions. In the case of Hungary his endeavors failed, for resolutions are not effective against a noncooperative superpower or its puppets.

United Nations resolutions follow public debates which in some instances are broadcast or televised. This brand of multilateral public diplomacy, similar to parliamentary debates, can be abused. In the ubiquitous battlefield of the Soviet and some Western powers, diplomacy by debate is often employed for propaganda purposes. Participation in debate by ignorant, mischevious, and malevolent delegates, some with unrealistic ambitions, constitutes a great hazard for parliamentary diplomacy.

These are some reasons why the virtues of this new kind of diplomacy are often disregarded, although diplomacy by conference has been used for the exposure of evil deeds and the promotion of world peace. In our era of mass communication, debates in the United Nations may influence public opinion in many countries and propaganda speeches may boomerang. But it is not easy to gauge public opinion in a single state, even if there is freedom of expression and there are public opinion polls. To assess a volatile and often uninterested world public opinion, and the possible effect of United Nations debates and resolutions, is a much greater task. World public opinion is composed of a multiplicity of heterogeneous and uncoordinated individual opinions, which on occasion may crystallize into sectional, regional, or professional views. In some countries opinion can be freely expressed but this is not the case in dictatorships. How can anyone know public opinion in countries which are isolated by iron, bamboo, or other curtains, and where there is no freedom of expression? Even in free countries the public often receives an oversimplified, if not distorted, picture of international problems.

Despite all these difficulties, we may assume the existence of a general opinion in civilized countries on certain fundamental human affairs. Such opinion is important in all states, and even dictators try to influence and measure it. Bulganin's and Khrushchev's famous letters to President Eisenhower regarding the summit meetings were for a worldwide audience. They appealed to the universal desire for peace. This was the rationale behind Stalin's peace campaigns. Both Stalin and Khrushchev as well as their successors realized that the desire for peace is one of the strongest political sentiments in the USSR as elsewhere. This partly explains why communist propaganda presents "Western imperialists" as warmongers. Although communist states exercise strong censorship and may jam foreign broadcasts, including those dealing with United Nations activities, in our era of mass communication important problems discussed before a worldwide audience can only be distorted, not totally suppressed. Individual opinions are beyond state control. It is possible to influence them from outside by proposals and speeches delivered at international forums, although the possibilities of influencing public opinion from abroad in dictatorships with institutional thought control is a difficult task.

United Nations debates are not transmitted in the same way to all member states, and much of the world's population is not informed of the United Nations' activities. In the Soviet Union, especially, only a few leading men can obtain full information on the outer world, including happenings in the world organization. The Soviet press republishes an edited version of Soviet addresses in the United Nations, and at most gives only a short and frequently distorted summary of other speeches and resolutions. United Nations publicity cannot easily pierce the intellectual iron curtain, and can hardly affect the picture of the world fabricated by the communist propaganda machine. The Soviet press creates the impression that the United Nations is a tool of American diplomacy. In reality, representatives of democratic states are under the control of public opinion, while communist representatives may freely make statements unrelated to fact as long as they are in harmony with the party line. Today full United Nations publicity exists only in the free world, while United Nations activities can have only a limited effect on people in totalitarian dictatorships.

The long-range effects of UN debates and resolutions on world public opinion admittedly belong to speculation. In politics intangibles can sometimes be more important than measurable things, and the United Nations as a world forum may have more importance, even in apparent failure, than is usually supposed. Struggle for the future is decided in the minds and hearts of men, a struggle for a life which will secure to a maximum of people happiness and satisfaction. Too much realism may result in narrow interpretation of national interests, and eventually may cause political blindness. Appeal to the heart is a necessity for which the open diplomacy of the United Nations should not be neglected. The General Assembly and other United Nations meetings constitute a forum where achievements of the West, and the negative sides of totalitarian systems, should come up again and again. The force of repetition is great and can help Western purposes.

A few Western states still carry the crippling legacy of colonialism, and the democratic states sometimes are divided on important issues,[10] but the general appeal of democracy is far greater than that of communism, as is demonstrated by the fact that in the strange Soviet semantics the word democracy has the same sense as communism. Since public debate and official statements at a world forum help expose fakery and falsehoods, diplomacy at the United Nations is more in harmony with democracies than with dictatorships. In the United Nations Soviet delegates several times overextended their propaganda hands and false Soviet statements underwent exposure before the world public.

Undoubtedly, democracies have on occasion been outsmarted by unscrupulous communist countries. But Muscovite propaganda in the United Nations was usually ineffective when contradicted by facts. Particularly in the early years of the United Nations, Soviet diplomats misjudged reactions of free nations to misrepresentation. Intemperate and false Soviet statements even helped make domestic opinion in the United States sympathetic toward a cooperative policy in world affairs and large-scale acceptance of responsibilities. Thus the open diplomacy of the United Nations provides a theater where Soviet diplomacy can not only be defeated but may defeat itself. God helps those who help themselves, and Western diplomacy should use the immense advantages offered by the United Nations. If Western states do not have a sound and dynamic policy, even self-defeating actions of Soviet diplomacy cannot be useful to Western interests.

No country is better fitted for open diplomacy than the United States, for foreign political questions have been openly debated in this country ever since its establishment. Now the debate embraces the whole world, where it is even more true that "you can't fool all the people all the time." The United States has many more ideas of universal appeal than does any other nation, but awareness of this by foreigners cannot be taken

---

[10] The late Ahmed S. Bokhari compared the European, Asian, and African attitudes in the following way: "It is true that neither Asia nor the Western countries can be regarded as a single political entity. But, whereas amongst the Asian and African nations there is, in spite of the diversity of governments, religions and races, a remarkable degree of unity on certain global issues, political and economic, the Western nations, in spite of their common legacies are split or are out of step with each other on almost all issues of world importance." "Parliaments, Priests and Prophets," *Foreign Affairs,* XXXV (April 1957), 409-10.

for granted. These ideas should be promoted through the United Nations, in competition for the uncommitted millions.

Parliamentary diplomacy in the United Nations is in its formative period. The United Nations is a convenient meeting place. Contacts can be made with a great number of states more easily and sometimes more successfully along the East River than through ordinary diplomatic channels. A great power can ascertain support for a policy. The hurly-burly of open meetings need not exclude confidential negotiations and consultations. The United Nations can help as an instrument for constructive action. Sometimes gaining time can be the useful objective of United Nations debates. Where national emotions are turbulent, some pressure can be channeled off through heated debate, while a "quiet diplomacy" may work out reasonable solutions. The vigorous role of the Secretary General is a milestone in the development of international organizations which has many possibilities for the future. While the Secretary General is using some of the best practices of traditional diplomacy in the interest of the world community, United Nations debates can act as catalyzers which direct emotions into placid waters. This is not a simple operation, to be sure, because delegates are greatly tempted to deliver addresses for popularity at home, and their imprudent speeches may inflame national sentiments.

All told, parliamentary diplomacy in the United Nations provides opportunities and channels for diplomacy that did not exist a few decades ago. It may facilitate cooperation, but cannot force states to cooperate. This new theater for world affairs requires the blending of diplomatic skill with the flair of a politician and the mobility of a newspaperman. Certainly, in parliamentary diplomacy different qualities are required of diplomats than in the usual bilateral diplomatic practice. Experiences in political and legislative affairs are most useful. The immediate rebuttal of Soviet accusations, practiced by Ambassador Henry Cabot Lodge and continued by his successors, Adlai Stevenson and Arthur Goldberg, is an example of how to use publicity in the General Assembly and Security Council for support of American policies. The Cuban missiles provided a good occasion to expose in a spectacular fashion the credibility of Soviet statements before a world audience. Stevenson performed his task with masterly art and the incident increased confidence in the United States. In some cases, however, silence is wisdom.

For settlement of important foreign political problems, bilateral diplomacy and *ad hoc* congresses with selected participants remain the normal diplomatic channels. Although the United Nations may perform functions in preparatory negotiation, the final agreement must be between states, for the General Assembly of the United Nations has no power to impose a decision. This fact is at the same time a source of danger, because popular imagination may attach exaggerated expectation to some United Nations activities and especially to resolutions which remain in the realm of verbalization unless supported by at least one superpower. A resolution accepted by a two-thirds majority in the Assembly is apt to create the illusion that a question has been solved, when in fact only a recommendation has been passed. Even dishonest policy, or lack of policy, can find temporary disguise in eloquence. Nevertheless, the virtues and shortcomings of a great power's foreign policy will have more effective exposition in the United Nations than through discreet diplomatic channels.

Parliamentary diplomacy in the United Nations is only a distant relative of traditional diplomacy, but the two often combine. Diplomacy necessarily has to operate within the power realities of a divided world. In view of basic ideological differences and conflicting national interests, United Nations meetings are sometimes transformed into battlefields where representatives of antagonistic governments argue vehemently. This is particularly true when conflicts are dominated by irrational emotions and fomented by antagonistic outside powers. Political differences may hinder cooperation even in such a technical organ as the Economic Commission for Europe. But the United Nations is not only a battleground. Representatives remain on speaking terms and in most cases a "quiet diplomacy" operates behind the scene. Early in 1949 the bar of the United Nations made possible a now famous meeting between Jacob Malik and Philip Jessup. In conversation the Soviet representative hinted that Moscow was willing to end the Berlin blockade. Contacts in the United Nations have made possible the solution of political conflicts and have even facilitated modest special cooperation between communist and noncommunist states—in exploration of Antarctica, in some cultural, scientific, and technical fields, in some aspects of outer space.

The specialized agencies and even the United Nations operate best in the economic, social, and technical fields—as was the case in the League of Nations. While in politics there are inexorable dividing lines between nations, in humanitarian fields the world community interest may more easily prevail. Many United Nations activities go on without Assembly action—except to vote funds—although cold war issues and other spectacular conflicts are much better publicized and dominate the public mind. Even in political matters, the United Nations has probably achieved more than seemed possible in the early postwar years.

The struggle for power remains a major factor in contemporary international politics. The world organization makes policy only in a limited sense; most of the time it is an instrument for the policy of national governments. The United Nations does not change the power realities of the contemporary world, nor does it hinder strengthening of the Alliance for Progress or the Western alliance system—particularly integration in Western Europe and partnership in the North Atlantic area. In some instances conflicts are highlighted by public diplomacy in the United Nations, but our major difficulties would still exist without the world organization. The Suez blunder occurred because the United States decided to make common cause with the Soviet Union and turn against the British and the French who, having lost confidence in American leadership, decided to act independently and without consultation of the American government. Solution of the Suez conflict was facilitated by the tranquilizing effect of United Nations action. Nasser and the Russians have accepted certain arrangements—such as occupation of strategic areas by United Nations peacekeeping forces—which otherwise would have been much less acceptable to them.

The United Nations has caused many disappointments in the United States, primarily because it was oversold to the American public. Expectations developed which had no basis either in the Charter or in political conditions of our time. Many official statements since 1945 emphasized that the United Nations was the cornerstone of American foreign policy. Such statements helped to foster the myth that if one simply "supported" the United Nations, the big problems of the world could somehow be solved. Victories in General Assembly voting were taken to mean that the United States was winning in international politics. Consequently, the American public has tended to overestimate the effects of United Nations resolutions and publicity, and even the opinions expressed in United Nations corridors. Too much reliance on the United Nations would mean abdication from United States responsibilities in world affairs, for, in vital matters, the United Nations is mainly a forum, not an agency. In reality, the United Nations in serious disputes can work out only temporary solutions. But even makeshift arrangements and postponement of conflicts constitute great achievements in our ideologically divided and rapidly changing world.

Diplomacy of Agencies
Related to the United Nations

During the last twenty years the advanced nations have been entering the scientific age, and there has been a prodigious multiplication of international technical agencies and institutions, partly on a world scale, partly in regional organizations. International agencies facilitated the development of communication and transportation, channelled economic aid and technical assistance to underdeveloped countries, supported fiscal and monetary reforms and promoted the liberalization of world trade and payments, and internationalized techniques connected with agriculture, production of food, and the peaceful use of fissionable material. Other international agencies spread knowledge across national boundaries about health, science, technology, labor, and education, and institutionalized activities in humanitarian fields.

The Charter has provided for regional arrangements in the system of the United Nations, and has created a specific organ, the Economic and Social Council (ECOSOC) for worldwide cooperation in the economic and social fields. Article 57 of the Charter provides that the "various specialized agencies, established by inter-governmental agreement and having wide international responsibilities . . . in economic, social, cultural, educational, health, and related fields, shall be brought into relationship with the United Nations in accordance with the provisions of Article 63." Article 63 states that ECOSOC "may enter into agreements" with any of the specialized agencies, "defining the terms on which the agency concerned shall be brought into relationship with the United Nations." The following inter-governmental organizations are linked with the United Nations by special agreements:

ILO—International Labor Organization

FAO—Food and Agriculture Organization of the United Nations

UNESCO—United Nations Educational, Scientific and Cultural Organization

WHO—World Health Organization

IBRD (Bank)—International Bank for Reconstruction and Development (World Bank)

IFC—International Finance Corporation ⎫
IDA—International Development Association ⎬ Affiliates of the Bank

IMF (Fund)—International Monetary Fund

ICAO—Internationl Civil Aviation Organization

UPU—Universal Postal Union

ITU—International Telecommunication Union

WMO—World Meteorological Organization

IMCO—Inter-Governmental Maritime Consultative Organization

IAEA—International Atomic Energy Agency[11]

ICITO—Interim Commission for the International Trade Organization

GATT—General Agreement on Tariffs and Trade[12]

---

[11] Although established "under the aegis of the United Nations," the IAEA is not a specialized agency as provided for by Articles 57 and 63 of the United Nations Charter.

[12] The Contracting Parties to the General Agreement on Tariffs and Trade (GATT)

Some agencies of the United Nations fulfill important functions in technical assistance, relief, humanitarian, and related fields. These agencies work in partnership with intergovernmental organizations.[13]

In addition to intergovernmental agencies, the Charter has made possible cooperation with private international organizations. Article 71 authorized ECOSOC to make "suitable arrangements for consultation with non-governmental organizations which are concerned with matters within its competence."

One of the consequences of these developments is that many problems formerly within the purview of government-to-government relations have come into the field of competence of international organizations. The specialized agencies have developed a new brand of diplomacy. Development of their special techniques has been influenced by the particular nature of their functions. Diplomats of national states may become members of the staffs of international agencies, may participate in conferences sponsored by these agencies, or may be accredited to them. Many draft conventions are prepared by international officials who have become special technicians of a new diplomatic art. The specialized agencies have worked out new techniques and new methods for dealing with contemporary international problems and for maintaining contacts with each other. There are several varieties of this new diplomacy which are adapted to the needs and functions of particular agencies. Within the scope of this study only a short summary can characterize these operational methods.

---

cooperate through the GATT secretariat, which was originally set up to serve as the secretariat of the Interim Commission for the International Trade Organization. (ITO has not been established and GATT is not a specialized agency.)

[13] United Nations Operating Agencies:

> UNDP—United Nations Development Program (United Nations, New York City, USA). [Established as a result of the merger of the Expanded Program of Technical Assistance and the Special Fund.]
>
> UNICEF—United Nations Children's Fund (United Nations, New York City, USA).
>
> UNRWA—United Nations Relief and Works Agency for Palestine Refugees in the Near East (Beirut, Lebanon).
>
> UNHCR—Office of the United Nations High Commissioner for Refugees (Geneva, Switzerland)
>
> UNCTAD—United Nations Conference on Trade and Development (Geneva, Switzerland)
>
> UNIDO—United Nations Organization for Industrial Development (Vienna, Austria)

Regional Economic Commissions:

> ECE—Economic Commission for Europe (Geneva, Switzerland).
>
> ECAFE—Economic Commission for Asia and the Far East (Bangkok, Thailand).
>
> ECLA—Economic Commission for Latin America (Santiago, Chile).
>
> ECA—Economic Commission for Africa (Addis Ababa, Ethiopia).

Most specialized agencies have a bureau for external relations which performs functions similar to those of a foreign office. An officer in charge of external relations maintains contacts with the United Nations, member governments, specialized agencies, and other intergovernmental organizations. Specialized agencies regularly send representatives to meetings of the other specialized agencies which concern them. They observe, report, and, if appropriate, participate in the discussion. Agreements are concluded by or under the authority of the executive head of an agency. The treaty-making power is only one indication that international agencies are subjects of international law. Executive officials of specialized agencies, for obvious reasons, regard it as a major part of their function to keep close contact with all member governments. An important problem in coordination is that often in member countries several national departments are responsible for the formulation of policies connected with the activities of the agency, and national governments themselves are not always coordinated.

The specialized agencies have created a new category of representatives in international relations in the form of the liaison officer, who is attached to another international organization and who works on the premises of the latter. He receives instructions and sends reports to his agency; usually an agreement on cooperation between the two agencies regulates his status.

The specialized agencies belong to the system of the United Nations, linked to it by a relationship agreement; they submit yearly reports to ECOSOC. The United Nations has certain functions in connection with specialized agencies and fulfills an important role as a clearinghouse. Nevertheless, the specialized agencies retain independence in policy, programming, and budget; they have an independent legal personality and could continue their activities even if the United Nations should cease to exist. Member states of a specialized agency are not necessarily members of the United Nations, and admission to the United Nations does not automatically involve membership in any specialized agency; but membership in the United Nations makes membership automatic in most specialized agencies if a state so desires. For example, Article 4 of the Constitution of WHO provides that members of the United Nations may become members of the World Health Organization by accepting the Constitution of WHO.

The treaty—sometimes called a constitution or statute—establishing a specialized agency determines the agency's goals, functions, and operational framework. A few specialized agencies adopted the system of "weighted" voting. This is of particular importance in the Bank Group (World Bank, IFC, and IDA) and the International Monetary Fund.

Since the budgets of the larger specialized agencies run into several millions of dollars, member governments keep a watchful eye on expenditures. The primary consideration in recruitment of international officials is the need to secure the highest standard of competence, efficiency, and integrity, but at the same time due regard is paid to the financial contribution of member states and to the necessity that the staff be drawn from various areas of the world. The new countries are anxious to have their nationals on the staff of international agencies, as a matter of prestige, a kind of status symbol, whether they have qualified men or not. But the desire to have nationals on the staff of international agencies is not limited to newly established countries. The great powers are particularly keen on having their nationals in responsible positions. Here it is not only a question of prestige, but has to do with the decision-making process of the organizations. In the older international agencies most positions were already filled when many of the developing countries were admitted and it was difficult for their nationals to get any kind of appointment. Directors of the agencies naturally try to hire the best specialists, but there are budget limitations and they have to consider the geographical principle. Compromises do not increase efficiency, and the problem is complicated by linguistic requirements. Another problem is connected with outside interference in the work of the secretariat. National governments can exercise pressure upon citizens serving on the staff of an international organization. Ideological commitments may cause further complications although in technical agencies political allegiance plays less of a role than it does elsewhere.[14] The degree and nature of difficulties connected with recruitment of personnel in international agencies vary. Member governments and administrators consider these difficulties as almost unavoidable.

Despite the different general objectives, several agencies have overlapping functions, some of which cannot be entirely eliminated. Although governments are against overlapping activities of international agencies, in some instances it may be desirable to have several agencies working on the same problems; such are the cases of scientific investigations, experiments, tests. In other instances the same subject is a natural part of the activities of

[14] See for the discussion of the role of Soviet personnel in international secretariats Alvin Z. Rubinstein, *The Soviets in International Organizations* (Princeton: Princeton University Press, 1964), pp. 254-88. For the general problems of international administration see Jerzy Stefan Langrod, *The International Civil Service* (Leyden Holland: A. W. Sythoff, 1963); Walter R. Sharp, *Field Administration in the United Nations System* (New York: Frederick A. Praeger, 1961); UNESCO, *Technique d International Conference* (Paris: UNESCO, 1951); Robert E. Asher *et al., The United Nations and Economic and Social Cooperation* (Washington: The Brookings Institution, 1957); John S. Stoessinger *et al., Financing the United Nations System* (Washington: The Brookings Institution, 1964); Mohammed Bedjaoui, *Fonction Publique Internationale et Influences Nationales* (New York: Frederick A. Praeger, 1958).

several agencies. Health is a major concern of WHO, but UNESCO is interested in medical training, biology, and health education, ILO is interested in social and occupational health, and IAEA has an interest in medical training, biology, and the development of water resources. Water concerns several other agencies—FAO, WHO, UNESCO, WMO, and the United Nations Water Resources Development Center. Of course, the focus of interest and approach of the agencies is different, but the basic material is water and the common subject may cause competition. Overlapping may come from interpretation of constitutions, sheer competition, and the influence of a peculiar Parkinson's law on international organizations. Since declarations of principle are not sufficient for genuine cooperation, the United Nations and the specialized agencies have devised the following instruments to secure cooperation and to eliminate overlapping, but since the specialized agencies are autonomous bodies, this process must be voluntary.

1. The Economic and Social Council of the United Nations "may coordinate the activities of the specialized agencies through consultation with and recommendations to such agencies and through recommendations to the General Assembly and to the Members of the United Nations" (Article 63, par. 2). All specialized agencies submit yearly reports to ECOSOC, including the agreements concluded. These reports give a general view of activities of the specialized agencies, and this facilitates the elimination of overlapping.

2. ECOSOC acted according to the spirit and letter of the Charter[15] in establishing an Administrative Committee on Coordination (ACC). Heads of the specialized agencies and some other international bodies, such as IAEA, GATT, and UNICEF, meet at least once a year under the chairmanship of the UN Secretary General to discuss practical measures for coordination and elimination of overlapping. There is also a Preparatory Committee of the ACC which discusses the problems of coordination in more detail. The ACC has set up a series of subcommittees in which the interested agencies participate. The fact that most specialized agencies have an officer of liaison in the United Nations facilitates the work of this Committee and the application of its recommendations.

3. A third form of coordination takes place through direct contacts, exchange of information, and documentation by the technical services concerned and the bureaus dealing with external affairs of the agencies. The chiefs of external relations have contacts with their colleagues in related agencies, and one of the major objectives of these contacts is program co-

[15] Article 58 provides that "The Organization shall make recommendations for the coordination of the policies and activities of the specialized agencies."

ordination. But program coordination is not always centered on the external relations divisions. Direct contacts of technicians working in related matters often are more significant.

4. A fourth form of coordination is in the field. Field coordination is the touchstone of the effectiveness of the cooperation agreements made by the central organs. In a capital such as Addis Ababa, more than a half dozen international agencies have projects. WHO is interested in health in general, UNICEF in the health of children. As these purposes are similar, a reasonable coordination must take place in the field where representatives of both agencies are aware of the needs and possibilities and are able to make economical use of the available funds. The United Nations Development Program coordinates the technical assistance and pre-investment work carried out under its aegis by the participating agencies and thus plays an important role in program coordination. A network of UNDP field representations has been set up. Under this system some eighty resident representatives coordinate the operational work of all the specialized agencies in a country or region.

Besides these categories of coordination, most specialized agencies have liaison offices in the United Nations and in several other specialized agencies. Two specialized agencies may agree on a common project or a particular form of cooperation. Most agencies send representatives to meetings of other agencies which are active within their fields of interest.

Political questions have disturbed the work of functional international organizations on many occasions. Suppression of the freedom of association of workers in Fascist Italy was the cause of lively debates in the ILO.[16] These discussions were resumed with greater vigor in ILO meetings in the 1950s when the Soviet Union and other communist states decided to join or reactivate their membership in technical organizations. More recently, the activities of strictly technical agencies have been overshadowed by purely political conflicts connected with racial and colonial policies, such as the exasperation of many new states against Portugal and the Republic of South Africa, whose participation in the work of most specialized agencies was the cause of objections by mainly the African, some Asian, and the communist states. This approach disregards the fact that the exclusion from participation in conferences of specialized agencies eliminates the possibility of negotiations and solutions of purely technical matters. Even such an apolitical specialized agency as the Universal Postal Union encountered political difficulties on the South African issue. The executive

---

[16] See Francis Graham Wilson, *Labor in the League System* (Stanford, California: Stanford University Press, 1934), pp. 16-20.

committee of the International Civil Aviation Organization proposed to expel the Republic of South Africa in July 1965. Subsequently the 15th session of the ICAO Assembly did not expel South Africa but passed a resolution condemning the policies of apartheid and racial discrimination practiced by that state.

A characteristic example of the political antagonism of our time was furnished at a conference sponsored by ITU, the oldest specialized agency.[17] At the African LF/MF Broadcasting Conference, convened by ITU in October 1964, the Algerian delegation requested the Conference to expel the representatives of Portugal and South Africa. This proposal was accepted by majority vote, but could not be carried out because the ITU Convention entitled all members to participate in conferences of the Union, and the Conference was suspended *sine die*. In view of this situation, in September 1965 the supreme authority of ITU, the Plenipotentiary Conference, decided to exclude from its meetings the Republic of South Africa. Subsequently, the Conference adopted a resolution sponsored by thirty-three African countries that the Republic of South Africa should not take part in ITU Regional Conferences for Africa and decided to reconvene the African LF/MF Broadcasting Conference for September 1966. Another resolution condemned the colonial policy of Portugal, but did not exclude the delegates of Portugal from ITU conferences.

There are a few technical agencies which have been able to work without interference of political disturbances. The history of the WMO is an interesting case in point. This agency came into being in 1951 as a specialized agency of the United Nations and is responsible for coordinating the development of networks of stations, with specified observational programs, to permit members to fulfill their responsibilities in the application of meteorology.[18] The worldwide character of the Organization is reflected in its membership which comprises 118 states and twelve territories. The fact that South Vietnam and South Korea are members, and that East Germany and Communist China are not, does not cause political complications, and the agency obtains data—directly or indirectly—from all over the globe, for cooperation is in the interest of the nonmember states as well. The work of this most useful agency[19] has not been disturbed by political conflicts.

---

[17] It was established in 1865 and had 131 members as of March 1967.

[18] The purpose of WMO, as laid down in Article 2 of its Convention, are to facilitate worldwide cooperation in the establishment of networks of meteorological stations and to promote the establishment of meteorological centers capable of providing meteorological services.

[19] At regular intervals weather stations throughout the world make meteorological observations at exactly the same time. The methods and practices followed are based on internationally agreed decisions and are practically uniform everywhere. Every day

WMO's collaboration with the United Nations covers general economic development, water resource development, and especially international cooperation in the peaceful uses of outer space. The agency maintains close and constant cooperation on numerous projects with FAO, UNESCO, ICAO, IMCO, ITU, and IAEA. With most member states administrative relations are carried on through the European Office of the United Nations, and in technical questions contact is maintained directly with the director of the meterological service in each country.

One of the unsolved problems remains the tendency to proliferate new autonomous organizations. This trend originates from the belief that the creation of a new international agency leads necessarily toward the solution of some specific problems. Although the establishment of a new agency may be necessary in some exceptional cases, proliferation is a wasteful approach which may aggravate existing overlappings and complicate solutions.

Complications caused by the establishment of new agencies was well demonstrated in the sessions of the Governing Body and the International Labor Conference of the ILO in 1966. In view of the gap between the national incomes of the rich and poor nations, ILO has been increasingly concerned with industrialization of underdeveloped countries and the social problems connected with it. In his report to the International Labor Conference, David A. Morse, the Director General of ILO, stated on June 21, 1966, that in 1965 the ILO implemented eighty-one technical cooperation projects in its major program of social institutions development, and forty-five projects in the major program of conditions of work and life. He pointed out that "nearly all these projects were designed to facilitate social adjustment involved in industrialization."

Meanwhile the General Assembly at its 20th Session authorized the establishment of the United Nations Organization for Industrial Development. Both the Governing Body and the International Labor Conference welcomed in 1966 the establishment of UNIDO and expressed their intention to cooperate with it, but the new situation apparently caused apprehensions. Morse stated in his report that "well-understood and clearly defined relationships must be established between the organizations of the United

---

about 8,000 land stations, 3,000 transport and reconnaissance aircraft, and 4,000 ships make 100,000 observations for the surface of the earth and 10,000 observations relating to the upper air. These figures are increasing from year to year as new stations are brought into service. WMO has adopted the international rules governing this work. Lists of weather stations, code manuals, and transmission schedules are issued by WMO and kept up to date by a regular and frequent service of supplements. They are used by meteorological services, airlines, ships, fishing vessels, and whalers. Some of the activities of WMO—particularly, measuring radioactivity in outer space—have significant implications for arms control.

Nations system to further industrialization." He also emphasized the necessity of coherent national policies with regard to coordination and full use of the services which the specialized organizations can offer. ILO's comments on the establishment of UNIDO are only an example of a general problem connected with the multiplication of international agencies.

By way of conclusion, one may say that the technical agencies have realized some of the global aspirations of mankind. Encouraged by their success, some scholars have suggested that conflicts can be gradually eliminated and mankind can reach the stage of "working peace" through functional cooperation.[20] This reasoning supposes that the cause of war is poverty, social injustice, backward industrial development, and other similar factors.[21] This supposition is not entirely correct. There is a political wall through which the specialized agencies and other technical organizations cannot penetrate. Racial hatred, jingo-nationalism, and aggressive ideologies are the major causes of conflicts. Political factors often hinder purely functional activities. The history of specialized agencies offers much evidence that a minimum understanding on basic purposes is necessary even for the satisfactory functioning of purely technical organizations. Nevertheless, the functional approach is a realistic method for cooperation in many fields. It is more important to light a candle than to curse the darkness. Functional organizations strengthen some special world community interests. Piecemeal successes in specific fields even on minor issues are more meaningful than agreements on lofty principles, which in practice mean different things to different nations.

[20] The chief protagonist of this school of thought, David Mitrany, developed his ideas in several publications. See *A Working Peace System* (London and New York: Royal Institute of International Affairs, 1946). For a balanced presentation of the problems involved in the functional approach to peace, see Inis L. Claude, Jr., *Swords into Plowshares,* 3rd ed. (New York: Random House, 1964) pp. 344–68 and James Patrick Sewell, *Functionalism and World Politics* (Princeton, N.J.: Princeton University Press, 1966).

[21] Prime Minister Attlee expressed this opinion at the opening session of the General Assembly in 1946: "In the purposes of the United Nations we have linked with the achievement of freedom from fear, the delivery of mankind from the peril of want. . . . Without social justice and security there is no real foundation for peace, for it is among the socially disinherited and those who have nothing to lose that the gangster and aggressor recruit their supporters.

"I believe, therefore, that important as is the work of the Security Council, no less vital is it to make the Economic and Social Council an effective international instrument. A police force is a necessary part of a civilized community, but the greater the social security and contentment of the population the less important is the police force." *Journal of the General Assembly* (January 11, 1946), p. 25.

SEVEN

New Forms of Diplomacy in Western Europe

While worldwide cooperation increased mainly in technical fields, the North Atlantic area and particularly Western Europe have developed new approaches for collaboration and integration on a regional basis. In an era of superpowers Europe has become weak and small. Two world wars destroyed its historical state system, and half of the continent passed under Soviet control. Despite these and other changes in Europe's relations to the rest of mankind, it was difficult to convince historically minded nations of the need for European integration. The sovereign state has been the basis of the European state system for centuries. Combined with the achievements of the industrial revolution, this system made Europe the powerhouse of the world.

Although from Dante's time many thinkers have put forward ideas for European unity, until recent years the idea of European political and economic integration did not occupy a prominent position in European politics. Unity of the old Roman Empire and the loose organization of the Christian Republic of the Middle Ages seemed parts of a bygone period. While in the United States between the world wars isolationism prevailed, Count Coudenhove-Kalergi's Pan-European movement was not much more than an exercise of a few European intellectuals. Briand's proposal in 1930 for a European Federal Union, endorsed by Edouard Herriot's book, *The United States of Europe,* likewise did not influence the course of European politics.

Pearl Harbor delivered a death blow to American isolationism. Then after the war, the Soviet threat created a new political climate on both sides of the North Atlantic which prevented isolationist policies. Stalin's aggressive policy facilitated the task of farsighted American statesmen. The United States abandoned traditional policies, and the formerly isolationist Congress approved measures which made possible permanent cooperation with European countries.

In the initial period of Atlantic cooperation and European integration the primary and probably the strongest driving force was the common danger. World War II gave way to years of frustration, Soviet troops remained in the heart of the Continent, and the Soviet Union imposed communist governments on nations in Eastern Europe. The rest of Europe lived in fear, uncertainty, and economic hardship. Western Europe, devastated by the war, was a major area destined for disintegration or unification. In his famous Zurich speech in 1946 Churchill described Europe's plight and then pointed out:

> Yet all the while there is a remedy which, if it were generally and spontaneously adopted, would as if by a miracle transform the whole scene, and would in a few years make all Europe, or the greater part of it, as free and as happy as Switzerland is to-day. What is this sovereign remedy? It is to re-create the European Family, or as much of it as we can, and provide it with a structure under which it can dwell in peace, in safety and in freedom. We must build a kind of United States of Europe. In this way only will hundreds of millions of toilers be able to regain the simple joys and hopes which make life worth living.[1]

The expansion of the Soviet Empire to Central Europe, the loss of most overseas possessions, and the emergence of new power centers on the globe gave sudden strength to the slogan "Europe, unite or perish." Moreover, it became clear that in an era of automation only large economic units are able to develop a modern industry which necessitates new scientific methods and particularly basic research on a gigantic scale. Despite these compelling factors, traditions of the European system, based on national states jealous of their sovereignty, proved to be strong and often obstructed reasonable responses to new challenges. Almost in all Western European countries some political leaders and intellectuals recognized the need for concerted action and unification; others were reluctant to change traditional views and refused to accept unorthodox approaches and policies. Some far-reaching goals were set, but the inability of politicians to adjust their thinking to the requirements of new world conditions caused serious setbacks.

The key area in Western Europe is a triangle formed by three highly

---

[1] Winston S. Churchill, *The Sinews of Peace* (London: Cassell and Company, Ltd., 1948), p. 199.

industrialized states: France, Britain, and Germany. The crux of Atlantic cooperation is also the Franco-German-British rapprochement and the harmonization of the policies of these three states with the objectives of American diplomacy. Interdependence is great between Europe and North America. The Atlantic Ocean has in a sense become smaller than the English Channel used to be. But states often take a strong stand for their immediate interests, real or imagined, and the other states react in kind. Short-sighted attitudes may defeat Atlantic purposes, and none of the Atlantic states would win in a conflict between themselves in the long run. Although in the early 1950s self-centered nationalism seemed to decrease, specific national considerations have remained important factors. This is the chief reason why, despite development of new diplomatic techniques for effective international cooperation and integration, the pace of integration did not become stronger with the passage of the years. The greatly watered-down structure of the Council of Europe is characteristic. Defeat of the European Defense Community in 1954, failure to unify Western Europe politically, and in particular the conflicts between France and her partners in the European Community and NATO are other examples.

Franco-German-British relations have been complicated by the participation of the three states in various international organizations, such as the United Nations (Germany has only an observer status), NATO, OECD, and numerous Western European regional bodies. In the last group the conflict between the federalists and the advocates of intergovernmental cooperation has remained a major problem. Germany, Italy, and the three Benelux countries prefer closer unity than the various British proposals or the Gaullist idea of *Europe des Patries*. Although Italy has made most impressive economic progress, she was unable to solve some of her difficult domestic problems, and to her the EEC means special advantages appreciated by all political parties including the communists. In the case of Belgium and the Netherlands a closer European unity means a compensation for the loss of colonies. Even after the transfer of the European Coal and Steel Community to Brussels, tiny Luxembourg remains the seat of the European Court and other international institutions. The small European states would particularly welcome a more active British participation in continental affairs.

As far as the methods of European unification are concerned, contemporary international conditions make almost meaningless the rigid interpretation of legal categories, such as federation and confederation. These distinctions developed in a different and much more legalistic world. The often quoted case of the German *Zollverein* and the subsequent creation of the German Empire or the development of the thirteen British colonies into a

United States of America are not wholly valid examples. Establishment of the German or the Italian national state meant the unification of a nation. The thirteen British colonies spoke the same language, and had the same cultural background. Their leaders were dissatisfied with the political system imposed on them by other Englishmen. Britain, France, Spain, and other Western European states have centuries-old independent existence. Their collaboration and the unification of some of their efforts is essential but methods applied in their case must be very different from those used in the past. The independent nationhood of European countries is a great asset for mankind. Endeavors to amalgamate them into a faceless federal state would be an unrewarding if not impossible task. It is difficult to visualize a European foreign ministry similar to the Department of State. But an independent foreign policy is not incompatible with the transfer of some important functions to international institutions. This has happened for the last one hundred years in limited fields. International organizations could make compulsory decisions within the fields of their jurisdiction. The contemporary European and world conditions present unprecedented challenges to which the European states should respond with increasing collaboration and even with transfer of power to international organs in some spheres which were formerly within the exclusive jurisdiction of national governments. In the light of European developments in recent years, the great debate between the advocates of a confederation and the federalists seems an almost futile intellectual exercise.

Problems of the crucial triangle and of the free European countries can be understood only from a broader perspective. After World War II the European countries had to face a series of urgent international problems. The liberalization of world trade which was successfully handled within the framework of GATT; the economic rehabilitation of war-torn Europe was carried out by the chief agent of the European Recovery Program, the Organization for European Economic Cooperation. In view of the Soviet threat, military security was provided by the Brussels Treaty (transformed in 1954 to the Western European Union) and primarily by the North Atlantic Treaty Organization. The Council of Europe provided a center for cooperation in political, cultural, and social matters. In the European Free Trade Association the member states abolished tariffs and other obstacles to trade among themselves, with minor exceptions, by January 1967, but each member retained its own tariffs toward non-EFTA countries. The innermost European circle was formed by the Six; these states decided to establish a common market, including a common external tariff and common solutions for some of their economic and social problems.

These organizations can be presented as concentric circles each of which fulfills different functions. The complex international problems of postwar Europe could not have been solved on the basis of traditional diplomatic practices. Imaginative Western statesmanship invented new approaches and methods which are not be be found in the annals of traditional diplomacy. Although successes of the new Western diplomacy particularly baffled the prophets of communism, the three crucial states, especially Britain and later France, were reluctant to proceed according to the requirements of present-day European conditions. Their attitude not only hindered further success but jeopardized Germany's definitive orientation toward a West European and Atlantic system.

Some of the new European organizations took over functions formerly handled through diplomatic channels, although diplomacy remained interwoven in many of their activities. The international agencies and institutions in Western Europe invented novel methods and forms for international business. Some institutions operate outside traditional diplomacy, and new diplomatic bodies and practices have been rising around them. In this respect, the Organization for European Economic Cooperation in particular has become a trailblazer which has produced most useful results.

THE ORGANIZATION FOR EUROPEAN ECONOMIC COOPERATION

The Organization for European Economic Cooperation (OEEC) and the Council of Europe have become prime symbols of Europe's revival. Both introduced new methods for the solution of international problems, affected European diplomacy, and developed useful models in worldwide relations.

Since political cooperation requires an agreement on some aspects of economic policies, it was fortunate that acceptance of the Marshall Plan preceded the North Atlantic Treaty Organization. Secretary Marshall in his famous address at Harvard on June 6, 1947, made the further American efforts to alleviate the European situation dependent on "some agreement among the countries of Europe as to the requirement of the situation and the part those countries themselves will take in order to give proper effect to whatever action might be undertaken" by the Government of the United States. He also suggested that "The program should be a joint one, agreed to by a number, if not all, European nations."

The European Recovery Program (ERP) was carried out in the spirit of Marshall's ideas. One of the products of the ERP was the Organization for European Economic Cooperation, which distributed the American aid, helped other aspects of the Program and worked out a code of liberalization of trade and other transactions. Over a period of four years the United States gave Western Europe $13 billion. A European Productivity Agency was established and its costs were paid by the United States. The OEEC became one of the most successful international institutions and continued its activities even after the cessation of American aid. It stimulated trade among European countries especially by the progressive abolition of quantitative import restrictions. Within the framework of OEEC the European Payments Union (EPU) facilitated international payments and provided credit facilities. The dollar gap was bridged. As most European countries introduced convertibility of currency, the EPU was replaced on December 27, 1958, by the European Monetary Agreement. The result was large-scale liberalization of European trade and a spectacular rehabilitation of European productivity. The Western European economy began to flourish.

Success of the ERP was greatly helped by a new economic diplomacy introduced by OEEC. In harmony with the Marshall Plan, the resources, plans and requirements of the participating states were examined and common policies worked out through direct confrontation of government officials and specialists. The economic interdependence of nations has long been recognized, particularly during economic crises, but the principles and methods have not been devised for effective action on the basis of inter-relatedness of economic interests. Methods inaugurated by the OEEC made possible practical cooperation in many fields.

The central organ of the OEEC was the Council, which had supreme authority for policy and administrative decisions. Composed of representatives of all member states, the Council met from time to time at the ministerial level and regularly at the permanent representative level. Its unanimous decisions were binding for all OEEC members. The member states established permanent delegations headed by ambassadors and thus a new diplomatic body, not accredited to the French Government, came into being in Paris. The diplomatic representatives met regularly once or twice a week and developed an *esprit de corps*. Diplomats who remained accredited for at least two to three years could contribute most to the work of the Agency. It was even more important that economic specialists and high-level officials of the member countries met regularly and agreed on advantageous economic policies. Technical committees were set up to deal with agriculture, transport, coal, steel, and other sectors of economic life. This new method of economic diplomacy has made possible the early acceptance of similar, if not identical, national policies. The operational methods of the OEEC and the diplomatic body accredited to it served as models for several international agencies in Western Europe, and leading officials of the OEEC have become prominent figures in other organizations.[2]

[2] Some of the examples are: Robert Marjolin, Secretary General of the OEEC from April 1948 to April 1955, who was appointed Vice-President of the EEC Commission

The OEEC proved useful in many ways. The Organization mediated between Britain and Iceland during their conflict over Iceland's extension of her territorial waters. As a result of OEEC mediation, the boycott of Icelandic ships established in two British ports in 1953 was abolished in 1956. This mediation by an economic organization between two NATO members illustrates the connection between the economic and political problems in our time.

The OEEC included seventeen European states (Austria, Belgium, Britain, Denmark, France, West Germany, Greece, Iceland, Ireland, Italy, Luxembourg, the Netherlands, Norway, Portugal, Sweden, Switzerland, and Turkey). Spain joined the OEEC in July, 1959. The United States and Canada had observer status, but in mid-1950 changed this status to that of associate members. Despite less than full membership, American representatives were intimately involved in the work of the OEEC, both on ambassadorial level and through day-to-day consultation of committees formed by the eighteen OEEC countries.

This participation proved a unique forum for cooperation between North American and European states. American representatives expressed their viewpoints with respect to the major economic problems of Western Europe and explained the reasons for American economic policies. Since all decisions in the OEEC had to be unanimous, voting was not necessary. The American views carried weight in discussions by virtue of United States initiative in organizing European economic recovery. European officials and American representatives collaborated in an atmosphere of mutual confidence. They understood each other's positions and the problems to be solved with an intimacy seldom achieved in international organizations. The United States wholeheartedly supported the objectives of the OEEC, in the belief that an economically strong Europe would contribute to the material welfare of the Western Hemisphere and to the ability of the Atlantic nations to build and maintain an adequate military defense.

Meanwhile, general European developments influenced OEEC policies. When six member countries decided upon the establishment of a Common Market, the OEEC Council appointed a working party in July 1956 to "study the possible forms and methods of association, on a multilateral basis, be-

on January 9, 1958; Guido Colonna, Deputy Secretary General of the OEEC from May 1948 to July 1956, later Deputy Secretary General of NATO, and since July 1964 a member of the EEC Commission; Frank E. Figgures, Director of the Finance and Trade Division of the OEEC (July 1948 to October 1951), who was appointed Secretary General of the European Free Trade Association in 1960; Milton Gilbert, Director of the Statistics and Economics Division of the OEEC (March 1951 to November 1960), who was appointed Financial Adviser to the Bank for International Settlements (BIS) in 1960.

tween the proposed Customs Union and member countries not taking part therein." The working party considered as a possible method of association the creation of a free trade area which would have included the Customs Union and the other OEEC member countries. The OEEC Council decided in February 1957 to begin negotiations for the creation of a European Free Trade Area, and in October 1957 OEEC appointed an intergovernmental committee under Reginald Maudling for the negotiation of the conditions of establishing a zone of free exchange. However, it was impossible to find a compromise solution between the Six and the other OEEC members. The failure of negotiations was recognized by the OEEC Council in December 1958, and subsequently the OEEC members decided to reduce the impact of Common Market discrimination through bilateral arrangements.

These events led to the creation of the European Free Trade Association under Britain's leadership in 1960. On the other hand, it was obvious that trade liberalization in the form introduced by OEEC was a great success but had reached the limits of its possibilities. As Europe was almost miraculously rehabilitated, the Western states turned attention to less fortunate regions. The highly industrial countries of Europe, North America, and Japan have a great deal to contribute to economic growth elsewhere. The important changes that have taken place in the international economic situation have been recognized in the communiqué of December 21, 1959, by the Heads of State and Government of France, the United States, the Federal Republic of Germany, and the United Kingdom. They agreed that virtually all of the industrialized part of the free world is now in a position to devote its energies in increased measure to new and important tasks of cooperative endeavor with the object of:

1. Furthering the development of the less developed countries, and
2. Pursuing trade policies directed to the sound use of economic resources and the maintenance of harmonious international relations, thus contributing to growth and stability in the world economy and to a general improvement in the standard of living.

The Organization for Economic Cooperation and Development

The Heads of State and Government recognized that the method of furthering these objectives requires intensive study and agreed to call a meeting in Paris. It was with this initiative in mind that Undersecretary of State Dillon made his proposals at the meeting of the Special Economic Committee in Paris, January 12-14, 1960, for reorganization of the OEEC into the OECD (Organization for Economic Cooperation and Development), for closer coordination of economic policies, trade and technical assistance, and full membership in the new organization for the United States and Canada. The word "European" was omitted from the title of the organization. Representatives of twenty nations signed the OECD treaty in Paris on December 14, 1960, and the new organization began to function on September 30, 1961. Its goals are to bolster economic growth and full employment in member states, to contribute to economic development in underdeveloped areas as well as in the treaty family, and to expand world trade on a multilateral and nondiscriminatory basis. The rule of unanimity continues.

The OECD has become "an international economic conference in permanent session." Japan acquired full membership in 1964, while Finland and Yugoslavia have a special associate status which entitles them to participate in certain OECD activities. Yugoslavia's participation is greater than that of Finland.

The OECD further developed the practice of direct confrontation of high government officials and leading specialists from member countries. Since all decisions of the OECD Council must be approved by unanimous vote, difficulties are eliminated on lower levels in committees and working parties. Scores of committees deal with major aspects of economic life, such as trade and payments, agriculture and fisheries, social problems and manpower, science and education, industry and energy. In committee meetings, reports and evaluations are followed by questions and comments by experts and high-level government officials. This process makes possible the development of common approaches and ways of thinking about complicated economic problems. In particular, monetary and fiscal problems can be solved more easily through close contact of the people who make policy. Mutual understanding among them is more important than formal agreement. Even after the meetings, the participants continue their discussions, criticize each other, and learn in this process.

The Economic Policy Committee in particular has become a *lieu de rencontre* of high-level officials who prepare policies in their country and make important decisions. Under the Economic Policy Committee operate three extremely efficient working parties. The working party on policies for the promotion of economic growth and the working party on costs of production and prices have full membership, while the working party on policies for the promotion of better equilibrium of international payments is restricted to ten countries. Representatives of Canada, France, Germany, Italy, the Netherlands, Sweden, Switzerland, Britain, the United States, and Japan meet normally every six to eight weeks, or more often if desirable. They discuss balance of payments and related problems, and the domestic and international measures necessary to deal with them.

Most of the time, the working parties bring together the same people, responsible civil servants in high positions. Resolutions are not formulated at these meetings, and there is no voting. But because the same people have to face each other time and again, a mutual trust develops and the given word is of great value. OECD did not institutionalize a rigid procedure for decision-making. Whenever member governments face urgent economic or financial problems, a meeting of leading officials is arranged. Members of embassies accredited to the OECD and the staff of OECD do not handle the merits of such issues. They have a directing and organizing task; they select and bring together people who are in the mainstream of decision-making in their national administration. Although OECD meetings are not for formal diplomatic negotiation, OECD methods represent some aspects of traditional diplomacy in a modern form. This procedure provides contacts among high-level government officials who receive much useful information about happenings, attitudes, and policies in other countries. The result is a better informed and more cooperative Western world.

The Economic Development and Review Committee prepares annual studies on the economic situation of each member country. The Secretariat sends detailed questionnaires to each member country in January. Country reports are discussed in the Secretariat and forwarded to two examining countries. Economists of the OECD staff and representatives of two examining countries draw up a list of questions which are discussed by special conferences arranged for each member state. Representatives from the country under examination answer the often delicate questions on problems, policies, and prospects of the nations concerned. The discussion that follows is conducted in a true spirit of give and take behind closed doors. In the light of all this information, the OECD staff under the direction of the chairman of the conference writes the final version of the annual study which contains factual analysis of the country's economic life and policy recommendations.

OECD also conducts surveys on some special problems. The Reviews of National Policies for Science and Education are concentrated on the development of human resources and stimulation of scientific and technological progress. According to the accepted procedure, a small team of examiners visits the country under review for discussion with officials, members of the scientific communities, representatives of industry, and other selected individuals and institutions. The observations of the examiners are included in a report which forms the basis for discussion at the confrontation meeting in OECD headquarters at the *Château de la Muette*. The country under review is represented by a delegation which participates in a round-table discussion with representatives of member states about questions raised by the examining team. Discussions are primarily on general policy questions, and thus the ensuing publication is useful for member and nonmember states alike.

One of the major objectives of OECD is to encourage and assist a balanced economic growth of the developing nations. The great challenge of our time is the creation of partnership between the rich nations in the northern and the poor nations in the southern hemisphere.

OECD includes the highly industrial states of North America, Western Europe, and Japan. Although the population of its member countries constitutes only 19 per cent of the world total, OECD member countries are responsible for 66 per cent of world industrial production; their international trade forms 71 per cent of world trade; they provide 90 per cent of the aid granted from all sources to developing countries.

Recognizing the urgency of assisting less developed countries, OEEC established the Development Assistance Group (DAG) in January 1960, when negotiations for the OECD were initiated. With the establishment of OECD, DAG was transformed into the Development Assistance Committee (DAC), the objectives of which are the increase of development aid and coordination of national assistance programs. The EEC is represented separately in the DAC. The United States, France, Britain, and the EEC are the four largest donors. DAC conducts country-by-country examinations of the volume, conditions, and financial terms, geographic distribution, and the purposes and techniques of the aid programs of the donor countries. Results of these examinations appear in a series of annual reports on "The Flow of Financial Resources to Developing Countries" and in the DAC Chairman's Annual Report. These reports are useful and have revealed fundamental weaknesses in the coordination of aid programs, one of which is the enormous accumulation of debt-servicing burdens in most underdeveloped countries. A growing number of governments feel that the reporting of quantitative data of aid programs is less important than the evaluation of the qualitative aspects of aid. The OECD Development Center, established in the spring of 1963, facilitates research on economic policy problems of developing nations and the training of their officials.[3]

Besides coordination and improvement of worldwide aid programs, OECD carries out modest aid programs for the benefit of its developing members.

[3] Some of the recent publications of the Development Center are Angus Maddison, *Foreign Skills and Technical Assistance in Economic Development* (Paris: Development Centre of the Organisation for Economic Cooperation and Development, 1965); Goran Ohlin, *Foreign Aid Policies Reconsidered* (Paris: Development Centre of the Organisation for Economic Cooperation and Development, 1966); Angus Maddison, Alexander Stavrianopoulos, Benjamin Higgins, *Foreign Skills and Technical Assistance in Greek Development* (Paris: Development Centre of the Organisation for Economic Cooperation and Development, 1966).

There is a technical assistance program for Spain, Greece, Portugal, Turkey, and Yugoslavia, and a financial aid program for Greece and Turkey. Moreover, member states may receive credits through the European Fund of the European Monetary Agreement. For example, in March 1965 the Council of OECD granted $70 million in credits to Turkey through the European Fund. This aid was to ease the servicing of Turkey's total external debt. Turkey's debts to the European Fund under previous credits totaled $95 million. During the period of these credits, Turkey's economic and financial situation will be under review by the appropriate bodies of OECD. In February 1966, Greece received $30 million credit. This was the eleventh credit granted by the European Fund. Besides Turkey and Greece, Iceland and Spain have received credits.

Because joint consultation and cooperation with other international organizations are mutually beneficial, OECD has established special relations with nineteen governmental and six nongovernmental organizations, as well as *ad hoc* contacts with a host of international bodies. OECD cooperates with FAO in connection with projects in agriculture, and with the International Monetary Fund in case of balance of payments difficulties of member countries. Manpower involves problems of education, occupational counselling, vocational training, social adaptation of workers to new conditions, labor-management relations, and the movement of manpower across national boundaries. In these matters the OECD maintains working relations with at least seven organizations.[4]

The OECD contributed to the development of an unprecedented collaboration and confidence among the major financial and economic powers. Nothing similar existed before World War II. Comparable cooperative efforts would have been unthinkable in the 1920s and 1930s. Even the most informed people did not have clear ideas of what governments of modern states could or could not do in economic and financial matters.

In recent years, unpublicized meetings of representatives of Central Banks and ranking financial officials created an atmosphere which prepared rescue operations of the International Monetary Fund. A remarkable international cooperation made possible the recovery of at least three currencies—the pound, the Canadian dollar, and the lira. Britain, in particular, received several massive financial transfusions from the Fund. Such operations followed an agreement of the group of ten to help the pound. They supplied the extra amount to the International Monetary Fund which made

---

[4] The European Economic Community, the Council of Europe, the International Labour Organization, the United Nations High Commissioner for Refugees, the Inter-Governmental Committee for European Migration, the Trade Union Advisory Committee, and the Business and Industry Advisory Committee.

possible the large loans to Britain. Prime Minister Wilson announced in February 1966 that Britain had already repaid more than half the assistance received from the Central Banks to surmount the balance of payments crisis in the spring of 1965. A few months later the pound was under pressure again and in June 1966 eight Central Banks from Western Europe, as well as from the United States, Canada, and Japan, agreed on a long-term arrangement to protect the British pound. Although the long-range solution of the inflationary trend and balance of payments problem in Britain depends mainly on the overhaul and modernization of the British economy, financial cooperation at least postponed monetary debacles.

Cooperation between OECD and the Monetary Fund is not restricted to the balance of payments difficulties of the member states, but includes aid for the developing countries, multilateral surveillance of international payments, and the study of monetary problems. In worldwide relations a reorganization of the system of international payments is urgent. Reforms are discussed and prepared by representatives of the group of ten. A new basis for international monetary policy should facilitate economic expansion throughout the Western world and increasing aid to underdeveloped countries.

EIGHT

The Diplomacy
of European Integration

Simultaneous with the diversification of international organizations in Western Europe and collaboration across the Atlantic, the style, scope, and technique of diplomacy was transformed with important effects on most fields of interstate relations. Functions were transferred from regular diplomatic channels to international bodies. Some traditionally bilateral procedures were shifted into the sphere of multilateralism. International agencies facilitated the solution of many trade and financial problems. Agreements on basic goals among the Atlantic nations facilitated the application of novel political and diplomatic patterns. Not only were the dimensions and methods of diplomacy adjusted to new needs by the OEEC and OECD, but this example was followed and in some respects paralleled by the Council of Europe, the North Atlantic Treaty Organization, the Western European Union, and other international bodies. A great variety of international organizations include most European and even extra-European states.

The inner circle of the European spectrum has been formed by France, Germany, Italy, Belgium, the Netherlands, and Luxembourg. The Six were willing to go further than the other states and set up the European Coal and Steel Community (ECSC) by the Treaty of Paris signed in 1951. The treaty transferred some of the powers of the contracting states to the High Authority of the ECSC and thus the first European organization with limited federal power was born in 1952.

The ECSC had been a great success by 1954 when the European Defense Community was defeated and the project for a European Political Community failed. Influenced by these developments, the Messina meeting of the representatives of the Six (1955) decided to relaunch the pattern of the ECSC in a broader framework; they proposed the economic integration of "Little Europe" and the development of sources of energy, both nuclear and nonnuclear. Subsequently, a study group under the Chairmanship of Paul-Henri Spaak proposed measures for the execution of the Messina ideas. Their proposals served as a basis for negotiations of the Common Market and Euratom treaties signed in Rome in March 1957, which established the European Economic Community (EEC) and the European Atomic Community (EURATOM) in 1958.

While the Treaty of Paris dealt with existing branches of industry, the EURATOM Treaty was concerned with an industry yet to be developed. Despite this important difference, both treaties are similar in the sense that they establish detailed rules to be applied within specific sectors of the economy of the Six. The EEC Treaty is quite different. It provides for the gradual merging of six separate markets into a single market with a common tariff within twelve to fifteen years. In connection with this process, the treaty contains some specific rules, particularly for the gradual elimination of customs duties and quantitative restrictions between member states. But in most other fields the Treaty only sets the goals and indicates the general lines of policy. The Community institutions have to formulate the specific measures necessary for the establishment of the economic union. Some of these measures are important laws for the six countries of "Little Europe" with far-reaching effects on their economic and social life.

The EEC treaty establishes an ingenious framework which makes possible organic growth without defining the nature of the association of the Six. This flexibility has left open the door for a variety of solutions in such important sectors as trade, agriculture, transportation, and, to a smaller extent, social policy. Understandably, the acceptance of a form of international legislation in these fields was often preceded by strong and critical debates and crises. The political feasibility of meshing the economies of the Six seemed doubtful on several occasions. It is a great achievement of Western statesmanship that important governmental functions of six sovereign states were progressively fused not only in trade and industry but that agreement was reached by July 1966, even for the fusion of all major segments of agriculture. Unification of agricultural prices and subsidy arrangements, that is, creation of a unified farm economy for Little Europe, was a particularly difficult task.

The European Communities are more than international organizations in the ordinarily accepted meaning of the term. They are institutions of specific nature without precedent in the history of international bodies. It would be difficult to define the proportions of intergovernmental and supranational elements, especially in the EEC which is still a developing institution. The traditional categories of confederation and federation cannot be applied either. The ambiguous French expression *"communautaire"* is probably the safest characterization of the Community system at the present stage of its development. Because political and economic questions cannot be separated entirely, full economic integration will require the harmonization of foreign policies and eventually the establishment of some federal institutions. This was the purpose of the European statesmen who participated in the Messina Conference in 1955 and signed the Treaties of Rome in 1957.

The Community system does not exclude closer collaboration among some member states. Benelux and the Franco-German Treaty of 1963 are cases in point. Although bilateral arrangements within the Community might defeat some basic *"communautaire"* purposes, the Franco-German Treaty was considered as a useful act for strengthening cooperation and friendship between two major and traditionally antagonistic states. Of course, conflicts must be avoided between the Community treaties and other multilateral or bilateral obligations of the member states.

Britain could have signed the treaties of Paris and Rome, but she did not want at that stage to adhere to European institutions with "federalist" implications. When members of the European Communities refused to accept the proposal concerning a loose free trade organization in Europe, she established with Sweden, Denmark, Norway, Austria, Switzerland, and Portugal the European Free Trade Association in 1960. The "Outer Seven" removed trade barriers among themselves, with minor exceptions, by December 1966, but they retained their own tariff structure in relations with non-EFTA countries. Finland joined EFTA as an associate member in 1961.

The organizational setting of the three European Communities is unique. Each of the three Communities has a separate executive body: the High Authority of the ECSC, the Commission of the EEC, and the Commission of EURATOM. All three of the Communities are served in common by the European Parliament and the Court of Justice. In the case of the ECSC, the High Authority has great freedom of action and the role of the Council of Ministers is very limited. In the EEC and EURATOM the Councils of Ministers make the major policy decisions based on the proposals of the executives. In some instances, before taking a formal decision, the Commission and Council must consult the Economic and Social Committee, which is composed of representatives of business and industry, farming, trade unions, and other interest groups.

The High Authority of the ECSC and the Commission of the EEC consist of nine members each, and the Commission of EURATOM of five members.

The Commissioners act as a collegiate body and cannot delegate some of their decision-making functions to a single Commissioner. Most decisions are made through written procedure and only the important questions are discussed at Commission meetings. The Commissioners appointed by common agreement of the member states perform their duties in the general interest of the Community with complete independence. But their re-appointment is subject to veto of any member state. Any government may oppose the appointment or re-appointment of a Commissioner irrespective of his nationality. For example, in 1962 the French government opposed the re-appointment of Etienne Hirsch, President of EURATOM Commission.

A treaty signed by the Six in 1965 provided for the merger of the two Commissions and the High Authority and the unification of the three Councils of Ministers. This treaty did not modify the powers and functions conferred on the original institutions by the Paris and Rome Treaties, but fused them into a single executive and into a single decision-making body. The Council agreed in April 1966 that the President and the three Vice-Presidents of the single Commission would normally be selected from the four major areas of the Community: Benelux, France, Germany, and Italy, and a partial agreement was reached on the rotation of the Vice-Presidents in the Presidency.

The new executive had been scheduled to take office on July 1, 1966, but the move was postponed, as no agreement had been made on the President of the single Commission. Most countries supported Walter Hallstein, who had been President of the Common Market Commission since its inception, but France opposed his candidacy. In this case the French veto maintained in office President Hallstein because members of the Commission remain in office as long as they are not replaced. When Hallstein declined an offer of short tenure, the Council of Ministers named Jean Rey of Belgium President of the single Commission effective July 1, 1967.

Because the High Authority and the Commissions are independent of the national governments, it is often suggested that in the European Community important decisions are actually made by a group of international officials, called Eurocrats, without serious parliamentary or other control. This is not the case. The Treaties of Paris and Rome delegated specific powers to the Executive as well as to the other organs of the Community. In every modern system the civil service has a great power, for most problems are of technical nature. It is also true that in a homogeneous international body officials may act more freely because of the clear understanding of goals, mutual aspirations, and means. In the Community administration highly competent people are confronted with extremely complex new problems and they have to find imaginative solutions. But this does not mean that they have entirely free hands. Actions of the Executive are authorized by treaty, and the Eurocrats are able to operate only within this framework.

The High Authority and the Commissioners are responsible to the European Parliament,[1] which has the power to dismiss them by a vote of censure carried by a two-thirds majority. In the event of important political proposals, the Parliament must be consulted before the Councils take any decisions. In addition to the six or seven one-week sessions a year, the various parliamentary committees secure quasi-permanent cooperation with the Commissions. Moreover, the members of Parliament may address questions to the various Community institutions. Both the questions and replies are published in the official Journal of the Communities. Up to the parliamentary year of 1965-66, 1042 questions were answered, as appears in the following statistic:

Parliamentary Year	58/59	59/60	60/61	61/62	62/63	63/64	64/65	65/66	58–66
EEC Comm.	12	61	80	75	146	135	132	104	745
EEC Council	5	2	5	6	8	6	8	5	45
EURATOM Comm.	6	6	13	3	5	11	7	3	54
EURATOM Council	5	1	2	–	4	2	3	–	17
High Authority	12	20	37	20	25	22	18	16	170
ECSC Council	1	2	3	–	1	–	3	1	11
Total	41	92	140	104	189	176	171	129	1042

Another guaranty of democratic control is the Court of Justice, which is the guardian of the Community law. It is composed of seven judges appointed for six years by common agreement of member governments. The Court ensures observance of law and justice in the interpretation and application of the Paris and Rome treaties. Its judgments are binding on Community institutions, member governments, corporations, and individuals.

While the Commissions represent Community interests and initiate Community policy, the Councils of Ministers are the decision-making organs of the Community. The Coordinating Committee of the ECSC, the Committee of the permanent representatives of the EEC and EURATOM, the special committees[2] and working groups with the assistance of the General Secretariat of the Council of Ministers—all contribute to the preparation of the de-

---

[1] See below, pp. 121–22.

[2] Article III of the EEC Treaty provides for the establishment of a special committee to assist the Commission in tariff negotiations with third countries concerning the common customs tariff. Another important special committee was created by the EEC Council for agriculture.

cision-making process of the Councils. The Councils of Ministers—like the European Parliament—has different functions *vis-à-vis* the three communities. In the ECSC the High Authority has substantial powers and the Council usually has only a consultative role, but on a few fundamental questions the High Authority's decision is not binding without the Council's approval. In the case of the EEC and EURATOM, the Commissions initiate and the Councils take the final decision in all matters of policy. The Councils can modify the proposals only by unanimous vote. However, the Councils may reject a proposal either by denying a weighted majority or in some cases because of a single negative vote. In the early stages the Rome Treaties required unanimous decisions which were gradually replaced by majority voting, although for a few fundamental policy questions, such as admission of new members or treaty amendment, the requirement of unanimity remains. Majority voting was extended to most important areas, such as trade, transport, agrarian and, in some rare instances, even social policy, from January 1966. For some questions majority vote was sufficient from the outset, and important member states, including France, Germany, and Italy, were voted down. For most majority decisions, votes are weighted: France, Germany, and Italy have four votes each, Belgium and the Netherlands two each, and Luxembourg one. Twelve votes constitute a majority. In some cases a government might prefer to be voted down rather than yield, because at home it might be easier to explain a defeat than a concession.

In January 1966 the Council of Ministers of EEC arrived at an "agreement to disagree" over the issue of majority voting. France, in effect, claimed the right of veto in the Council of Ministers on those issues which she feels affect her "very important" interests. The other five member states, while supporting the principle of majority voting, pledged themselves to attempt to reach unanimity over a reasonable period of time before taking a majority vote. This attitude was in harmony with the practice of the Council and it meant the rejection of the French position. A conflict of more general nature exists between France and the Five. France advocates a strict interpretation of the Treaty of Rome with respect to the power of the EEC Commission. The Five, in turn, would like to give broad and flexible power to the Commission in order to facilitate the development of the Community.

The Council of Ministers has proven to be a remarkably effective instrument in the process of the harmonization of national interests. Its decisions are directly binding on their member states, individuals, and corporate bodies. The Commission and Council may adopt regulations of general validity in the Community or they may issue directives to one or more member states. They also may express opinions or formulate recommendations without binding force or take decisions addressed to a government, corporate body, or individual.

Since the Council meetings are secret,[3] the Council escapes from pressure group action while in session. In some instances the governments of the member states could not have adopted measures which domestic considerations might have made politically impossible if the Council's decisions had not been made.

One of the shortcomings of the Community machinery is the lack of capacity to make rapid decisions in some questions related to foreign affairs. The process of formulating a proposal and securing a Council decision can be frustratingly long in a world where events move rapidly. The United States witnessed the slowness of the Community's decision-making process during the 1963 poultry dispute and later in connection with the Kennedy Round of tariff negotiations. In 1965 the French boycott blocked all three Communities' decisions for seven months. The Community situation may become particularly frustrating for diplomats of outside powers who are accustomed to negotiate with states within the framework of established policies and procedures. Although they have informal contacts with the permanent representatives, it is practically impossible for them to meet the real decision-makers, the Ministers, during the brief Council meetings in Brussels. The diplomatic contacts with member states are made through embassies in the six capitals.

Sixty-nine states had accredited missions to EEC, twenty-eight to ECSC, and twenty-seven to EURATOM as of March 1967. A government wishing to establish diplomatic relations with the Community has to inform the Commission; the Commission examines the request and after approval forwards it to the Council, which normally approves or disapproves the proposal within thirty days. A similar procedure is followed in the case of accreditation of chiefs of mission. This twofold procedure made possible a curious incident in the case of Nationalist China.[4] The duly approved chiefs of mission presented their credentials to the President of the Commission in style. The laborious ceremony established for the reception of the newly accredited heads of mission by President Hallstein created resentment, particularly in France. Although accreditation is a function shared by the

[3] In 1962 there were 65 Council meeting days; in 1963, 66; in 1964, 71½; and in 1965, 35. Because of the French boycott, the Council could not meet for seven months in 1965.

[4] The Council approved the establishment of diplomatic relations with the Chiang Kai-shek Government, but shortly afterward France recognized the People's Republic of China and the French representative in the Council vetoed the accreditation of the representative proposed by the Nationalist Chinese Government.

Commission and the Council, after the ceremonies of accreditation several diplomats did not even pay the expected courtesy visit to the President of the Council of Ministers. As President Hallstein received the new diplomats with a certain solemnity, the French Government suspected that the purpose of the elaborate protocol was to enhance the supranational character of the EEC and refused to approve accreditation until the number of designated chiefs of mission grew to seventeen. The Council agreed in January 1966 that the credentials of chiefs of mission should be presented to the President of the Commission and the President of the Council. Finally, in July 1966, a new procedure was arranged according to which the credentials are presented the same day but separately to the President of the Commission and the President of the Council, and France agreed to the accreditation of the seventeen heads of mission. In the case of the ECSC, the High Authority alone accredits the heads of diplomatic missions. Seniority in the diplomatic body accredited to the EEC, EURATOM, and ECSC is determined by the date of presentation of credentials.[5]

Missions accredited to the European Community are organized as regular diplomatic establishments and perform the usual diplomatic functions: they observe, report, negotiate, and try to influence the Community to adopt a policy favorable to their countries. Since there is no public opinion in the ordinary sense, the missions try to influence the Community institutions. Contacts are made with the Department of External Relations and the technical Departments of the Commission and with leading executive officials, but the missions try to exert influence through several other channels as well, and maintain a wide variety of informal contacts. Large missions may send observers to the sessions of the European Parliament to buttonhole politicians in the lounge in the same manner as in the United Nations. A mission to the Community usually receives copies of the instructions sent by the foreign minister to the embassies accredited to the Six. In a similar way, the regular embassies in the six community states share their diplomatic reports and other relevant information with the mission of their country accredited to the Community. Members of the diplomatic missions accredited to the Community enjoy the usual diplomatic immunities and privileges and form a separate diplomatic body, although the same persons may be accredited to the Belgian or other governments as well as to the Community.

The six member states have permanent representations in Brussels, each of which is headed by an ambassador. These delegations have a quasi-

---

[5] The United States accredited an ambassador to the ECSC in 1952 as the head of the American Mission. The same ambassador was accredited to the EEC and EURATOM in 1958, when the Mission moved from Luxembourg to Brussels.

diplomatic character. They are parts of the Community system and form the permanent bureau of the Ministers who represent their countries in the Council. The permanent representatives fulfill an important liaison function in interpreting the aims and methods of the Community executives to their governments. There is a vast and endless exchange of information and opinions among the six governments and with the Community executives. The permanent delegations play a central role in this process. Moreover, they participate in the work of various Community institutions.

The Councils of Ministers at their first session in January 1958 established, on the basis of the treaties of Rome (Art. 151 of EEC and Art. 121 of EURATOM), the Committee of Permanent Representatives which is composed of representatives of member states. The Committee has regular sessions almost each week.[6] They prepare the subject matter for each Council meeting, but they do not have decision-making power; they are not deputies of the Council of Ministers. However, many agreements worked out at the permanent representative level are simply rubber-stamped by the Councils. If unanimous agreement is reached between the six permanent representatives and the representatives of the Commissions in questions of lesser importance, the Councils usually take decision without discussion.

The treaty-making activity of the Communities developed in several directions. The ECSC concluded a consultation agreement with Switzerland and a customs tariff agreement with Austria. The EEC concluded commercial treaties with Lebanon, Israel, and Iran. Greece and Turkey became associated with the EEC by separate agreements, signed in 1961 and 1963, respectively. Both agreements provide not only for a customs union but for the gradual establishment of full membership in the EEC when the economies of the two states permit them to assume all of the obligations of the Treaty of Rome.

The Six agreed in Article 131 of the Treaty establishing EEC "to bring into association with the Community the non-European countries and territories which have special relations with Belgium, France, Italy and the Netherlands." After independence, seventeen African states and Madagascar[7] decided to continue the association agreement which was contracted for them by European countries in 1957. The Second Association Convention, signed at Yaoundé in 1963, went into effect on July 1, 1964, for

---

[6] In 1962 there were 107 meeting days, 108 in 1963, 120 in 1964 and 106 in 1965. See for the best discussion of the role of this important organ, Emil Noel, "The Committee of Permanent Representatives," *Journal of Common Market Studies,* Vol. V (March 1967), 219-251.

[7] Burundi, Cameroun, Central African Republic, Chad, Congo (Brazzaville), Congo (Kinasha), Dahomey, Gabon, Ivory Coast, Madagascar, Mali, Mauritania, Niger, Rwanda, Senegal, Somalia, Togo, Upper Volta.

a period of five years. The Association means the creation of a free trade area between the Six and the associated states with substantial protection for the developing industries of the African associates. Under the agreements the associates receive grants, technical aid, and special loans,[8] and their products enjoy preferential entry to the Common Market.

In July 1966 Nigeria signed a Treaty of Association with EEC. The terms of the association are important because they may pave the way for other English-speaking African states to associate with the Common Market. Nigeria gained by the agreement tariff-free entry for all her major agricultural products, but the volume was restricted to the level of these exports to the six EEC countries during a previous three-year period,[9] and she does not receive development aid. Nigeria has granted duty-free entrance on only twenty-six products of the six EEC countries. The agreement allowed Nigeria to maintain her special relations with Britain, the Commonwealth, and EFTA countries.

Representatives of the seventeen African states and Madagascar, and of the two European associated states, have an ambiguous status. They are in the list of diplomatic missions, but in certain relationships covered by the treaty of association they act almost as the representatives of member states. Representatives of the associated states are called "Permanent Delegates," in contradistinction to the "Permanent Representatives" of member states.

The Council of Association consists of the EEC Council of Ministers, the Commission, and one representative each from the associated countries. This Council meets once a year. The routine administration of the Association Convention is carried out by the Association Committee, composed of one representative from each of the Community countries and the associated countries.

The Community has not established missions abroad, though there are some plans for this. Only the ECSC has a mission in Britain in view of a special agreement of association concluded with the British Government in 1954. Austria and Switzerland have also signed agreements with the ECSC. The three Communities have established information bureaus in all member states and other important countries. Moreover, they maintain close relations with numerous international bodies, the activities of which are connected with their task.

---

[8] Under the first five-year association agreement the Community provided, through the European Development Fund (EDF), aid totalling $581 million. The second association agreement increased this amount to $730 million, to which the European Investmen Bank added $70 million.

[9] This restriction was imposed because the French-speaking African associates feared that Nigeria might swamp Little Europe with the same products they export duty-free.

EURATOM is linked with virtually all the European national projects and international agencies for the peaceful application of fission and fusion by association contracts, liaison committees, and other contacts for cooperation and exchange of information. EURATOM has especially close relations with the European Nuclear Energy Agency (ENEA), established by the OECD. The Commission sends representatives to meetings of the Board of Governors of the International Atomic Energy Agency, the International Labor Organization, the United Nations Food and Agricultural Organization, the Inter American Nuclear Energy Commission, and the Council of Europe. EURATOM signed an agreement with the United States for a joint power station program and a joint research and development program (1958), with Britain for exchange of information and cooperation (1959), with Canada for joint research, and with Brazil and Argentina for cooperation over a wide field of activities (1961 and 1962). EURATOM concluded a supplementary agreement with the United States in 1960, which was amended in 1963. The new agreement provides for the supply of uranium-235, plutonium, and uranium-233 to the Community. The United States Atomic Energy Commission signed an agreement with the EURATOM Commission in 1964 covering a vast program of cooperation on fast reactors. There are plans for cooperation on the field of heavy water-organic liquid reactors.

The seat of the European Free Trade Association is at Geneva, but each EFTA country has a mission accredited to the European Community in Brussels. Once a month a high official of the EFTA Secretariat goes to Brussels and has a meeting, followed by informal conversations with the heads of mission of the eight EFTA countries. Contacts and some sort of accommodation between the EEC and EFTA countries are most important in order to avoid the dangers likely to result from the existence of two different economic groupings of countries in Western Europe. There are regular meetings for exchange of information between the General Secretariat of EFTA and officials of the Commission of EEC, and there is some coordination of activities in a few technical fields. Since the EFTA countries established a free trade zone by January 1, 1967, and the EEC will strip away on July 1, 1968, the remaining tariff barriers, an economic boundary will split Western Europe into two camps. EFTA emerged as a free trade area of approximately 100 million people who would face 185 million inhabitants of the Six. Such an artificial division of the most developed European nations seems a self-defeating exercise, as it would have particularly wasteful effects on investments and Europe's resources would be squandered unnecessarily. Thoughtful men both in EEC and EFTA countries are aware of the untoward economic and political consequences of such developments and are endeavoring to improve relations between the two groups. But this is not a simple process because it cannot be done without clarification of some underlying policies and approaches of the two associations.

Agreement reached by the Six on major agricultural prices and subsidies in July 1966 made possible for the EEC a meaningful participation in the Kennedy Round tariff-cutting negotiations. Success of the Kennedy Round will lower the barriers to trade, both worldwide and in Europe, and thus facilitate trade between EEC and EFTA groups until the establishment of a comprehensive European economic system.

What are the general interests of Europe in contrast to the particular interests of individual states or groups of states? Which state or group of states should make sacrifices for higher community interests, and who is competent to make decisions in cases of interest conflict? Only the EEC has a machinery which may resolve such problems within the Community by majority vote. But even there France (her treaty obligations notwithstanding) challenged this process in 1965, and after a seven-month boycott, reserved the right to veto the decisions in important questions. At the present stage of European development, clarification of interest conflicts and many related problems must be made through diplomacy, and for this difficult task numerous new channels are available.

The large number of diplomatic missions accredited to the European Community is unique in the sense that a large number of nonmember states have accredited missions to the three Communities, while in most other cases only member states accredit missions to an international organization. Under the new conditions of the North Atlantic area, not only has the size of most foreign ministries and embassies increased rapidly, but even the diplomatic bodies have multiplied. Decades ago two *corps diplomatiques* existed only in Rome, one accredited to the Italian Government, the other to the Holy See. During the 1920s and 1930s member states accredited missions to the League of Nations, and Geneva became a new center of diplomatic activities. Since World War II new diplomatic bodies accredited to international organizations have been mushrooming. In Paris there were three diplomatic bodies, one accredited to the French Government, and the others accredited to NATO and OECD respectively. Other *corps diplomatiques* were accredited to the Council of Europe (Strasbourg), the Western European Union (London), the International Atomic Energy Agency (Vienna), the European Office of the United Nations, the European Free Trade Association (Geneva), the Food and Agriculture Organization (Rome), and the three European Communities (Brussels).

These developments have influenced diplomatic methods; some functions which formed part of regular diplomacy were transferred to international agencies. Most of the new international organizations and institutions do not belong to any traditional legal category, such as federation and confederation. They are new creations of the post-World War II era. In some relations their success or failure is more important for the future of Europe than the traditional functions of diplomats, although international institutions and traditional diplomacy will have to coexist for many years to come, even if by miracle a United States of Europe could be established. Some major characteristics of the new Atlantic diplomacy can be summed up as follows.

1. Simultaneous with multiplication of diplomatic bodies, the size of diplomatic establishments has greatly increased, and they have undergone transformations. The embassies of great powers include representatives of major government agencies, and the business of diplomacy embraces most human activities. It should be noted, parenthetically, that the growth and diversification of diplomatic personnel is especially conspicuous in the case of the United States. The ambassador's task often requires the versatility of a jack-of-all-trades. Concentration on pure politics in a traditional sense belongs to history. Economic and related social problems have become important.

2. Conditions in the North Atlantic area often necessitate change from bilateral to multilateral negotiations. The growth of international organizations illustrates the fact that interstate business is done increasingly through international agencies. Consequently, diplomacy has become not only multilateral, but collective. The scope of the work of international officials has broadened, and their importance has increased.

3. The work of regional and functional organizations includes large-scale research, and their publications are helpful not only to the Atlantic nations. This is true even in the case of some politically handicapped organizations. The political division of Europe restricts the activities of the United Nations Economic Commission for Europe (ECE), but the vast amount of information the Commission collects from official sources and publishes is useful on both sides of the iron curtain.[10]

4. Cabinet members, responsible government officials, and leading experts of national states meet regularly within the framework of an international agency, and in many cases they create common understanding of international problems and agreement on policies and procedures. Formal intergovernmental agreement may follow their understanding.

---

[10] David Wightman, *Economic Cooperation in Europe: A Study of the United Nations Economic Commission for Europe* (New York: Frederick A. Praeger, 1956). ECE endeavors to work out rules which may facilitate East-West trade expansion.

5. Interest groups participate in the international policy- and decision-making process either as organized pressure groups and political parties or as consultative organs of some European institutions, such as the Economic and Social Committee of the EEC.

6. Several European international institutions established since World War II have a hybrid character. This is a manifestation of difficulties underlying the process of European unification. European unity cannot be achieved according to traditional procedures and legal concepts, such as confederation and federation. Many intermediate solutions are accepted, and the result is in some cases a studied lack of clarity of institutional settings, procedures, and methods.

7. Experience has demonstrated that even modest steps have their own momentum, called the spill-over effect, if supported by the *cognoscenti* and the public. Under favorable conditions, the spill-over effect acts as a powerful force for further collaboration and integration.

8. The cumulative effect of the activities of international organizations and institutions is slowly transforming the national societies and the structure of government and administration.[11]

9. In each member state of EEC, Community law coexists with municipal law. This situation necessitates cooperation between the Court of Justice and the domestic courts. After some hesitation, it has been accepted that where there is conflict, Community law should prevail.[12] Existence of a Community law restricts the scope of diplomacy.

10. Lastly, the proliferation of international assemblies is a peculiar characteristic of postwar developments. This phenomenon warrants a more detailed examination.

INTERNATIONAL PARLIAMENTS

Since World War I parliamentarians have actively participated in the international business of governments. Parliamentarians in democratic countries became increasingly interested in external affairs in the late nineteenth century. They desired to discuss international problems with their

[11] See for discussion of some of the problems involved: Max Beloff, *New Dimensions in Foreign Policy—A Study in British Administrative Experience, 1947–1959* (New York: The Macmillan Company, 1961); *Les Conséquences d'Ordre Interne de la Participation de la Belgique aux Organisations Internationales* (Bruxelles: Institut Royal des Relations Internationales, 1964). This book was prepared by an interuniversity study group appointed by the Institut Royal des Relations Internationales.

[12] For the Community legal system, see *Ninth Annual Report on the Activities of the Community* (EEC Commission, June 1966) pp. 349–62.

colleagues of foreign lands and this aspiration led to the foundation of the Interparliamentary Union in 1889.[13] After World War I they were often heads or members of government delegations sent to the Assembly of the League of Nations. Their participation in public diplomacy and international negotiations has become part of the diplomatic scene. These practices were followed by most democratic states after World War II. In the United Nations numerous delegations include parliamentarians from both government and opposition parties. Of course, parliamentarians have to act according to instructions as long as they are members of a government delegation. American Congressmen and Congressional Committees frequently travel abroad as independent observers, but this practice, a reflection of worldwide United States responsibilities, has little imitation in foreign countries. Similar but more limited practices exist in France, Britain, Germany, and other countries with parlimentary government.

In Western Europe the growth of international organizations and institutions has created problems for parliamentary democracies. It is one of the consequences of contemporary conditions that even in democracies the power of the executive has greatly increased. The transfer of numerous governmental functions to international organizations not only diminished the role of traditional diplomacy, but also contributed to the further weakening of parliamentary control over the executive. The debate and decision-making processes often take place within the organs of international organizations, as we have seen in the case of the OEEC and OECD. In the EEC officials of the Commission, the Eurocrats, prepare solutions for many important economic problems on the basis of the Treaty of Rome. The acceptance of their proposals by the Council of Ministers in reality often means legislation. The major immediate cause of conflict between France and her partners in the EEC in June 1965 was a proposal made by the Commission for the strengthening of the budgetary powers of the European Parliament.[14] On this occasion the French representative in the Council of Ministers rejected the Commission's proposal. In most instances, however, international officials work out proposals for the solution of specific problems

---

[13] In several instances politicians initiated negotiations for the solution of conflicts at conferences of the Interparliamentary Union. Such *prise de contact* took place between the German and Israelite politicians in 1951 concerning the compensation for damages caused by the Hitler regime to the Jews. Later the Italian and Yugoslav politicians established direct contact with respect to the Trieste conflict. English and Egyptian politicians used the Conference of the Interparliamentary Union in 1957 to begin informal negotiations for the settlement of the Suez issue.

[14] See for details, Leon N. Lindberg, "The Role of the European Parliament in an Emerging European Community," in *Lawmakers in a Changing World,* ed. Elke Frank (Englewood Cliffs, N.J.: Prentice-Hall, Inc., 1966), pp. 101-28.

in cooperation with high-level government officials and specialists of member countries. If they agree on the best solution, the member governments usually endorse the proposal.

In view of the close cooperation between national and international officials, a fear exists that the national executives and pressure groups may use international institutions for the dispossession of parliaments. National parliaments may have the power to reject agreements reached through the decision-making process of international bodies, but in practice parliamentary debates and control may be reduced to sheer formalities.

It is desirable to avoid situations which would frustrate national parliaments. Most international agencies welcome visits of parliamentarians from member countries and are willing to have contacts with them in any reasonable way. But private contacts are not sufficient. Creation of international parliaments is one of the means to assure democratic control over international agencies. If parliamentarians participate in the early stage of negotiation, and are consulted by international officials, they are able to influence the international decision-making process, and a feeling of frustration does not develop in national parliaments. Besides these general considerations, there were specific reasons why six international parliamentary assemblies were established in the following order:

1949	Consultative Assembly of the Council of Europe
1952	Common Assembly of the ECSC. This was replaced in February 1958 by the European Parliamentary Assembly of the ECSC, EEC and EURATOM. The Assembly adopted the name European Parliament in March 1962.
1953	Nordic Council
1954	Consultative Assembly of the Western European Union
1955	Conference of NATO Parliamentarians
1957	Benelux Interparliamentary Consultative Council

If these parliamentary assemblies have different origins, compositions, and functions, they also have some common features. All of them are responses to new needs in Western Europe and the North Atlantic area. Through international assemblies politicians have systematic contacts with their colleagues from foreign countries and with international officials; and at the same time they have established new theaters for international debates where they operate in a familiar parliamentary environment.[15]

[15] See for details Kenneth Lindsay, *Toward a European Parliament* (Strasbourg: Secretariat of the Council of Europe, 1958); Kenneth Lindsay, *European Assemblies: The Experimental Period, 1949-1959* (New York: Frederick A. Praeger, 1960); J. Allan Hovey, Jr., *The Superparliaments—Interparliamentary Consultation and Atlantic Cooperation* (New York: Frederick A. Praeger, 1966).

The European Parliament has well-defined functions, including ultimate control over the executive of the three European Communities. Its 142 members are elected by the national parliaments of member states.[16] France, Germany, and Italy elect thirty-six members each; Belgium and the Netherlands fourteen each, and Luxembourg six. The executive must submit a yearly report to the European Parliament which has the power to oust the executive by a motion of censure, voted by a two-thirds majority. In case of the High Authority a motion of censure can be expressed only in connection with the examination of its annual report. The Commissions of EEC and EURATOM must resign any time if a motion of censure is adopted by a two-thirds majority of the Parliament.

Members of the European Parliament sit in alphabetical order, within their political group, irrespective of nationality. At the outset three political groups were formed: the Christian Democrats, the Socialists, and the Liberals and associated parties. An amendment to the rules of procedure in January 1965 provided that a group must consist of at least fourteen members, aligned by political affiliation irrespective of nationality. This amendment enabled the French Gaullist deputies, members of the "Union for a New Republic" (UNR) to constitute a separate group, the European Democratic Union. In 1966, the Christian Democratic group had sixty-one members, the Socialist group thirty-five, the Liberal group twenty-six, and the European Democratic Union fifteen. Members meet according to their political affiliation, and each of the four groups have permanent secretariats.

The thirteen Committees of the Parliament prepare reports for the plenary sessions and maintain quasi-permanent relations with the executive. The Commissions discuss most problems with the Committees. This continuity in contacts makes it possible for the executive to clear policy proposals informally with the Parliament before their formal submission to the Council of Ministers.

Cooperation between the Council of Ministers and the Parliament is facilitated by annual "colloquies" between the two institutions. The Council does not submit a yearly report to the Parliament but customarily the President of the Council once or twice a year gives a verbal account to the Parliament of the major activities of the Council in the preceding months.

A convention between the European Parliament and the associated African countries and Madagascar provided for a Parliamentary Conference of the Association consisting of fifty-four members of the European Parliament and three representatives from each of the Parliaments of the 18

---

[16] A draft agreement on the election of the European Parliament by direct universal suffrage was submitted to the Council of Ministers in June 1960, but action was not taken by member governments.

associated African nations and Madagascar. The Conference met for the first time at Dakar in 1964. Parliamentary bodies were formed by the European Parliament and the Greek Assembly, on the one hand, and the European Parliament and the Great National Assembly of Turkey on the other, to secure parliamentary control over the activities of the association of Greece and Turkey with EEC. The joint yearly session between the Council of Europe and the European Parliament establishes contact between the parliamentarians of the Six and of the Eighteen.

In contrast to the well-defined functions of the European Parliament, the Consultative Assembly of the Council of Europe is a town meeting of European parliamentarians without much power or direct political authority in any specific area. Since federalist ideas did not prevail in Strasbourg, the Council of Europe could not become a political authority. Nevertheless, the Council of Europe provided a center for cooperation in political, cultural, social, and legal matters, and in the protection of human rights. Although the Assembly has power only to discuss and make recommendations to the Committee of Ministers, it has been called, with some euphemism, "the general framework of European policy." [17]

The number of parliamentarians of the eighteen member countries is roughly proportional to population. France, Germany, Italy, and Britain have eighteen representatives each, Turkey ten, Belgium, Greece, and the Netherlands seven, Austria, Switzerland, and Sweden six, Denmark and Norway five, Ireland four, Cyprus, Iceland, Luxembourg, and Malta three.[18]

It is a feature of the Consultative Assembly that each parliamentarian may have a substitute who may sit, speak, and vote in his absence. Members sit in alphabetical order and usually vote according to party lines. In many countries the national parliaments elect the "Representatives to the Assembly"; in others, such as Britain, the government appoints them in consultation with the political parties through the Party Whips; in both cases, the national delegations are composed in proportion to the distribution of parliamentary seats between the different parties. The Statute of the Council authorizes the Assembly to discuss almost any questions, with the exception of matters relating to national defense. The Assembly has, in fact, discussed and made recommendations even on defense, and the Committee of Ministers has not objected to discussions in the Assembly

---

[17] See for details the standard work by A. H. Robertson, *The Council of Europe*, 2nd ed., (New York: Frederick A. Praeger, 1961); Ernest B. Haas, *Consensus Formation in the Council of Europe* (Berkeley: University of California Press, 1960).

[18] Spain and Portugal participate in several technical organizations of the Council but are not members.

of the political aspects of "European peace and security." [19] Cabinet ministers frequently attend the Assembly meetings; they may use the Strasbourg forum for important policy statements, and also have opportunity to argue their case directly with parliamentarians of their own and other countries.

The Consultative Assembly made possible for the first time a transnational parliamentary cooperation of political parties and the clarification of views on specific issues through international parliamentary debates. Christian Democrats, Social Democrats, Liberals, and members of other parties represented similar interests in various countries. They understood each other and were able to conduct meaningful discussions within the framework of the Council of Europe. Most of them supported the trend for European unification, but there were great differences between the "federalist" and "functionalist" approaches.

Many fruitful ideas—mainly in cultural, social, legal, and functional fields —originated in the discussions of the Assembly and were subsequently embodied in recommendations to the Committee of Ministers. This is the executive organ of the Council of Europe and consists of the foreign ministers of the Member States. One result of these activities was the conclusion of nearly fifty treaties of European interest. By December 1966 the exact number was fifty-four, but five are only of internal interest— dealing with privileges and immunities. Some deal with social security and medical assistance, others with peaceful settlement of disputes, establishment, extradition, television program exchanges, equivalence of diplomas, and various cultural matters and medical subjects.

The first and probably most important treaty initiated by the Council was the European Convention for the Protection of Human Rights and Fundamental Freedoms, by which the contracting parties guaranteed to all persons within their jurisdiction a number of rights and freedoms and established a Commission of Human Rights and a European Court of Human Rights to make sure that the guarantee would be effective. The Convention entered into force in 1953, and members of the Commission were elected in 1954 for a period of six years. The Court of Human Rights was established in 1958 and fifteen judges were elected; the number is now eighteen. In the Convention on Human Rights states undertook legal obligations to respect the civil and political rights to all persons within their jurisdiction; another innovation is that it permits individuals to appeal to an international body (the Commission of Human Rights) even against

---

[19] Since the establishment of the Western European Union and the NATO Parliamentarians' Conference in 1955, there are two special organizations where questions connected with defense are debated.

their own governments. By the end of 1966 the Commission had received 3,000 individual applications. Another instrument of major importance was the European Social Charter, concluded in 1961, which deals with economic and social rights.

The organization of local authorities represented an unprecedented development. The Consultative Assembly accepted a proposal to convene a European Conference on Local Authorities. The Committee of Ministers agreed that it should meet every two years and in 1961 approved the Charter of the Conference by which it received permanent status. Conferences of Local Authorities have been instruments for European integration in practical terms. Participants discuss problems, learn from each other, and create grass-root understanding among nations. Such meetings serve unity more than high-level declarations of principle.

Economic and social developments are strongly influenced by science and technology. Science in our time represents a major activity on which the well-being of nations depends. Still, there is little direct contact between scientists and policy-makers. The European Parliamentary and Scientific Conferences established liaison between them. The first conference was in London in 1961, the second in Vienna in 1964. These conferences were jointly sponsored by the OECD and the Council of Europe. The Council invited the parliamentarians, and the OECD the scientists.[20] Other conferences organized by the Council of Europe are the Conference of Ministers of Education and the Conference of Ministers of Justice, each of which meets every two years.

The Council cooperates with several European international organizations and maintains relations with nonmember states. Important international organizations, such as the European Communities, the International Labor Organization, and most specialized agencies, send annual reports to the Council of Europe. The Assembly discusses the reports and may make recommendations in the form of resolutions and address them to the organizations concerned. It may approve or criticize some of their activities. Thus, in a broad sense, the Assembly exercises parliamentary review over international organizations active in Europe. The Council of Europe has concluded agreements or made arrangements with numerous international organizations—such as the United Nations, ILO, UNESCO, WHO —concerning exchange of information, consultation, and exchange of ob-

---

[20] The European Parliamentary and Scientific Conferences are most important because basic and applied research is much more developed in the United States and in the Soviet Union than in Western Europe. C. Freeman and A. Young, *The Research and Development Effort in Western Europe, North America and the Soviet Union.* (Paris: Organisation for Economic Cooperation and Development, 1965).

servers. All member states have accredited permanent representatives to the Council of Europe. They are the deputies of the Ministers and they have regular monthly meetings.

The Assembly of the Western European Union[21] (WEU) has an official status and meets twice a year in Paris. Its primary task is to debate defense problems and the annual report of the WEU Council; it has power to make recommendations to the Council composed of the foreign ministers of member countries. The same eighty-nine parliamentarians who represent their countries in the Council of Europe are members of the Assembly of the WEU. The Assembly and its committees often discuss general political problems and thus may duplicate discussions in the Council of Europe. The scope of the discussions, however, cannot be restricted in view of the broad objectives of the Brussels Treaty and the provisions of the Charter of the Assembly. ("The Assembly carries out the parliamentary functions arising from the application of the Brussels Treaty.") WEU is the only organization which includes Britain and the Six alone. It was in the Assembly of WEU that the first official proposals were made for the accession of the United Kingdom to the European Communities. Nevertheless, WEU is handled in the European family of international organizations rather as a poor relative. The sessions of its Assembly create only limited interests because most topics of general importance are debated in the Council of Europe and defense problems in the Conference of NATO Parliamentarians.

It is paradoxical that the Conference of NATO Parliamentarians, though a private organization, is considered politically more influential than the official Assembly of WEU. Of course, the Conference of NATO Parliamentarians is the only political forum where American and European parliamentarians meet and engage in public debates about defense questions and the related public policy. Addresses by military commanders and prominent political leaders enhance the importance of the Conference. In contrast to the European assemblies, the NATO Parliamentarians' Conference was not established by treaty, but by an agreement among the national legislatures of NATO countries. Voting in the NATO Parliamentarians' Conference is by national delegation on the basis of a unit rule. Each delegation is assigned a specified number of votes regardless of the actual size of the delegation. Out of a total vote of 175 the United States has 36 votes, Canada 10, and for the European members the number of votes is the same as in the Assembly of the Council of Europe.

[21] Paul Borcier, *The Political Role of the Assembly of the W.E.U.* (Paris: Western European Union, 1963); Assembly of the Western European Union, *Ten Years of Seven-Power Europe* (Paris: Western European Union, 1964). See p. 134 for details.

Since 1955, Parliamentarians from NATO countries have met yearly; their recommendations are important in clarifying the trends for future developments. In London in June 1959 the Conference organized an Atlantic Congress for the tenth anniversary of NATO. This Congress created an Atlantic Institute in Paris and launched plans for an official convention which was convened in Paris in January 1962 for the exploration of greater cooperation and unity of purpose within the Alliance. The convention proposed developing the NATO Parliamentarians' Conference into a Consultative Assembly, establishing an Atlantic High Court of Justice and strengthening the Atlantic Council.

The future of the NATO Parliamentarians' Conference depends on NATO's reorganization. A different NATO might need an official Parliamentary Assembly, or else the meetings of parliamentarians might become superfluous. The development of an Atlantic Community would necessarily include a parliamentary assembly with well-defined functions. But the American Congress and political trends in Europe do not seem to point toward the realization of such bold reforms in the near future.

The Nordic Council consists of members of parliaments elected by the legislative assemblies of Finland, Sweden, Norway, Denmark, and Iceland, and of representatives of the governments of these five nations. The parliaments of Denmark, Finland, Norway, and Sweden each elect sixteen members, and Iceland sends five members to the Council, which thus has sixty-nine members. The Council meets once a year, and a session usually lasts from seven to ten days. For each session the governments appoint as many cabinet ministers as seem necessary with regard to the subjects considered. They participate in debates, but do not vote.

The Nordic Council can discuss any question of common interest but cannot take a binding decision. This is a body for consultation. The Council has no joint secretariat, but each country has a permanent secretariat. Planning of a session is the responsibility of the secretariat in the country where the coming session is to be held. Each session elects a Presidium in charge of the Council's work until the next session. The Presidium consists of a president and four vice-presidents who are the leaders of national delegations to a session.

Cooperation among the Scandinavian states has been traditional in social and cultural matters, as in communications, traffic, and other technical fields. The Nordic Council has systematically coordinated these efforts and facilitated a close cooperation among legislative assemblies and governments. This has been a remarkable achievement, for the positions of the five member states have been different in the international political arena. Sweden maintained her traditional neutralist position; Finland concluded a treaty of friendship, cooperation, and mutual assistance with the Soviet Union in 1948; in the following year Denmark, Iceland, and Norway joined NATO. Thus the Scandinavian countries of necessity are members of different political groups, but through the Nordic Council they try to coordinate their policies in the UN, UNESCO, FAO, OECD, GATT, and other international organizations.

The Benelux Interparliamentary Consultative Council has advisory competence in broad fields which include not only the establishment and operation of an economic union among Belgium, the Netherlands, and Luxembourg, and closer cultural relations among them, but even cooperation in foreign policy and the unification of law in the three states. The three governments may, by joint agreement, consult the Council on draft conventions among the three member states relating to these matters or other matters of common interest.

The Council is composed of forty-nine members who are appointed by the Belgian (21), Dutch (21), and the Luxembourgian (7) parliaments. Decisions of the Council, expressing an opinion usually in the form of a recommendation, are made by a two-thirds majority. Each year the Council receives a joint report from the governments on questions within its competence. Members of the three governments or other persons designated by them may attend the meetings of the Council and may speak there. The participating states consider Benelux a genuine success.

Although international parliaments take an important part in Western European cooperation, they have remained in the sphere of a special branch of diplomacy. None of them fulfills genuine international legislative functions. Several parliaments facilitate the close contacts of parliamentarians with international agencies. What is perhaps even more important, international officials, politicians, and high officials of numerous nations meet regularly at international assemblies and thus have occasion to work together and possibly to know and trust each other. Harold Macmillan, Heinrich von Brentano, Guy Mollet, and some other leading politicians were members at the same time of the Political Committee of the Council of Europe. In the EEC there is an almost permanent consultation between the Commission and the organs of the Council of Ministers on the one hand, and the Committees of the European Parliament on the other. In several assemblies the ministers themselves participate in parliamentary debates and may reflect on the presentations of parliamentarians of their own country and of other countries. The similar cultural backgrounds of the European nations facilitate meaningful debate and agreement on political objectives.

But the contribution of international parliaments to Western cooperation is not an unmixed blessing. Parliaments are organs of entangled international organizations, several of which are results more of makeshift arrangements than of rational planning. One may even argue that the multitude of international organizations has become a source of confusion in their duplications and overlappings. As we have seen, some of the objectives of the WEU are similar to those of the Council of Europe and NATO. Either the WEU Assembly must restrict itself to the discussion of disarmament and other special questions or it duplicates the debates of other international parliaments. However, overlappings and even contradictions in the structure of international organizations are perhaps unavoidable at this stage of European development. An organizational reform would not be simple because the membership is not the same in the various international organizations, and neutral states could not risk political involvement. Slack organizations reflect the reality of the European situation.

Logically, gradual and systematic integration would be preferable for the political unity of Europe. It is easier to create international parliaments with limited purposes in small geographic areas among cooperative nations; the Nordic Council and Benelux are cases in point. Some advocates of the gradual process suggest that it would have been better to establish first WEU and later the Council of Europe. According to this school of thought, it is difficult to coordinate the policies of seven states, and it is infinitely more complicated to do this with fifteen or twenty states. This approach is correct mathematically, but in politics mathematics and logic do not always apply. It is most important that statesmen act at an appropriate moment, for which they need sound judgment and impulses. Once the historical momentum is lost, it may never return. Several variations of mergers and rationalizations of international organizations have been suggested, such as the merger of the OEEC with the Council of Europe. It is not difficult to create ideal institutions on paper, but it is questionable whether these would solve complex problems of economic and political life. One could marshal arguments for a unified European Parliament and even for a trans-Atlantic Assembly with the inclusion of parliamentarians from the United States and Canada.

While it is easy to make bold proposals, at the present time only the European Parliament has ultimate control over the executive, and none of the existing international assemblies has legislative power. They are special instruments of a new kind of diplomacy rather than genuine parliaments. Substantial reforms and rationalization of international organizations must accompany the consolidation of international assemblies in Western Europe.

Over and above the organizational problems looms the unity of foreign policy. Institutions and organizations cannot hang in the air. They reflect the reality of political conditions, and they must serve some common political or economic purposes. Organizational perfection is not a substitute for agreed policies. Structures and functions could be improved and assemblies unified, but functional rationalization would not be a substitute for the determination to establish a political community in Europe. The first practical step could be a better organization of European states on a regional basis.

In bilateral diplomacy states are trying unashamedly to promote their own national interests. In international institutions and organizations a community type of diplomacy should develop with concentration on community interests. Here the great difficulty is clear definition and acceptance of community interests. A major problem remains that economic cooperation must be in harmony with basic political purposes. The success of economic cooperation or union is not an answer to the final goal, which is political unity in essentials. Multilateral diplomacy and international institutions may play an important role if governments are willing to use them. In recent years a setback occurred in this respect because Gaullist diplomacy preferred bilateral agreements and even unilateral actions. Nevertheless, the general trend of international developments remains. The Western European international organizations have great merits. With their help—and also thanks to prudential use of the more than $20 billion American economic aid—the ingenuity and industry of the Western European nations have changed the desperate postwar economic situation. Europe has become again a power factor in international politics. The habit of cooperation in economic matters may facilitate the gradual development of a common foreign policy for Europe and the Atlantic area.

In our interdependent world, economic, political, and military security interact. Economic and social progress would not have been possible in an atmosphere of subversion and Soviet aggression. The political security so necessary to constructive social and economic endeavors was brought about by the American military guarantee to Western Europe through the North Atlantic Treaty Organization.

NINE

NATO Diplomacy

Institutional Developments

The revival of postwar American diplomacy began in 1947 with the policy of containment. Defensive diplomatic moves were initiated from unfavorable positions. Despite handicaps and long-standing isolationist traditions, the United States proved able to answer new challenges, though sometimes haltingly. The Truman Doctrine saved Greece and Turkey from communist subversion and Soviet domination. The Marshall Plan saved Europe from economic chaos.

Then came outright political measures. The Senate's acceptance of the Vandenberg Resolution in June 1948, by an overwhelming vote of 64 to 4, showed that this body, strongly isolationist on the eve of World War II, now recognized the new American responsibilities in world affairs and was willing to act in a flexible way and in a spirit that disregarded old political traditions. The resolution recommended association of the United States with "regional and other collective arrangements for individual and collective self-defense" under Article 51 of the United Nations Charter. American foreign policy produced the North Atlantic Treaty and other multilateral and bilateral defensive agreements. NATO's protective shield, and particularly the American retaliatory capacity, greatly improved the political and psychological climate and brought to Europe a measure of self-confidence and stability. There followed the spectacular total recovery of Western Europe—unprecedented economic growth, a new era of cooperation, and some integration in the North Atlantic area.

The structure of NATO underwent several transformations. Its predecessor in Western Europe was the Brussels Treaty of March 1948, signed by France, the United Kingdom, Belgium, the Netherlands, and Luxembourg.

The North Atlantic Treaty, which consists of fourteen concise articles, was signed in Washington on April 4, 1949, by the United States, Canada, Denmark, Iceland, Norway, Italy, Portugal, and the five signatories of the Brussels Treaty. Soviet actions in Eastern Europe, particularly the communist seizure of power in Prague in February 1948 and the Berlin blockade in 1948-1949, gave impetus to these developments. Shortly after the establishment of NATO the explosion of an atomic bomb by the Soviet Union had a further effect on Western military considerations, although the actual change in the balance of power occurred only in the early 1950s when Soviet operational capabilities in the atomic field became evident. NATO's ability to carry out a new Western strategy became enormously important when the Anglo-American atomic monopoly ended.

The treaty of 1949 established a defensive alliance which is authorized by Article 51 of the Charter of the United Nations. Although an armed attack against any one of the contracting parties is "an attack against them all," NATO's purpose is broader than military defense of the geographic area defined in Article 6 of the treaty. Members must "safeguard the freedom, common heritage and civilization of their peoples, founded on the principles of democracy, individual liberty and the rule of law." These objectives have followed from realization that Soviet imperialism does not restrict itself to any area and does not use only military means for expansion.

Before the communist aggression in Korea in 1950, the North Atlantic Council had met three times and concentrated on establishment of military and civil bodies. The highest military organ, the Military Committee, consists of the chiefs of staff of member countries. The Standing Group is the executive agency of the Military Committee; its members were representatives of France, the United Kingdom, and the United States. France withdrew her representative on October 1, 1966.

Since the cost of modern armaments has been prohibitive for most NATO allies, Washington has become the major provider of military equipment. Shortly after the Mutual Defense Assistance Program began, the outbreak of the Korean War greatly influenced NATO. In June 1950 the Western nations realized that what had happened in Korea could happen in Germany. NATO's strategy had been based on defense of the Rhine-Ijseel line, which implied evacuation of Germany east of the Rhine and of the northern part of the Netherlands. The Dutch representative called this plan "plain lunacy" and advocated defense of Germany at the session of NATO Council in September 1950.[1] Obviously, a "forward strategy" was not realistic without German participation, as fourteen Western divisions, faced by

[1] Dirk U. Stikker, *Men of Responsibility,* p. 298.

175 Soviet divisions, were hardly adequate. In addition to satellite divisions of doubtful value, the Soviet Union had 125 divisions in immediate reserve. In the Council there was unanimous agreement to create "an integrated force under a centralized command, adequate to deter aggression and to ensure the defense of Western Europe." Secretary of State Acheson argued for German participation in Europe's defense, but France objected—a position in harmony with a strong anti-German policy followed by France in the early postwar years. The principle of German participation in the common defense was accepted at the Council meeting the following December. The French government worked out a scheme for "a European Army linked to the political institutions of a United Europe," and Premier René Pleven submitted the plan to the French Assembly in October 1950. The Pleven Plan provided for a European Minister of Defense responsible to a European Assembly and "a complete fusion of all the human and material elements" of the proposed army. The European Defense Community (EDC) finally met defeat in the French Parliament in August 1954,[2] and the German Federal Republic did not enter NATO until May 1955. Meanwhile, defense of NATO's southeastern flank was secured when Greece and Turkey joined NATO in February 1952.

Under the influence of the Korean War and the continuing communist threat, and through its own organic growth, NATO has become much more than a simple alliance. The functions of the North Atlantic Council and its subordinate organs and the position of the secretary general are without precedent in the history of international organizations. NATO is unique even as a military alliance, for it has within its framework in peacetime unified military commands, composed of representatives from member countries.

The NATO area has three Commands and a Regional Planning Group. Allied Command Europe extends from the North Cape to North Africa and from the Atlantic to the eastern border of Turkey, excluding the United Kingdom and Portugal. (Defense of the latter countries remains a national responsibility.) The Supreme Allied Commander Europe has four subordinate commands—one each in the northern, central, and southern parts of Europe, and one in the Mediterranean. Allied Command Atlantic extends from the North Pole to the Tropic of Cancer and from the coastal waters of North America to those of Europe and Africa, including Portuguese waters and the islands in the area such as Iceland and the Azores,

---

[2] See Herbert Luethy, *France Against Herself* (New York: Frederick A. Praeger, 1955); Alexander Werth, *France 1940-1955* (New York: Holt, Rinehart & Winston, Inc., 1958); Raymond Aron and Daniel Lerner, eds., *France Defeats EDC* (New York: Frederick A. Praeger, 1957); Edgar S. Furniss, Jr., *France: Troubled Ally* (New York: Harper & Row, Publishers, Inc., 1960).

excluding the British Isles and the Channel. The Channel Committee and the Channel Command cover the English Channel and the southern part of the North Sea. Strategy for defense of North America is prepared by the Canada-United States Regional Planning Group.

The Council appointed General Dwight D. Eisenhower as Supreme Commander of Allied Forces in Europe (SACEUR) in December 1950, and he established Supreme Headquarters Allied Powers, Europe (SHAPE) near Paris and began to organize a coordinated NATO army for defense of the NATO land area in Europe. This work went on under his successors, the American Generals Matthew B. Ridgway, Alfred M. Gruenther, Lauris Norstad, and Lyman L. Lemnitzer.

The great advantage of NATO is its well-organized command structure, its instantaneous communication and radar systems, and its preparedness for many contingencies. In our time an old-fashioned alliance treaty would not be satisfactory. It is doubtful whether an operation plan for coordinated Allied actions could work in an emergency. Experience in both world wars supports this contention. Integrated command does not mean integration of national armies.[3] It means that reasonable military plans for contingencies are devised by an international staff, and that military maneuvers take place periodically. NATO's organization has made possible a kind of military preparedness which would not exist in a simple alliance.

The limit of each member's contribution to military readiness and the measure and form of American aid to members of NATO have become highly controversial subjects. The purpose of the organization would be undermined if military expenditures of its member nations were to cause economic and social setbacks. These problems came under discussion at the Ottawa meeting of the Council in September 1951, when for the first time foreign ministers, defense ministers, and economic or finance ministers represented member states. This meeting appointed a Temporary Council Committee (TCC) of the "three wise men"—Averell Harriman from the United States, Jean Monnet from France, and Sir Edwin Plowden from the United Kingdom—"to survey urgently the requirements of external security, and particularly of fulfilling a militarily acceptable NATO plan for the defense of Western Europe, and the realistic political-economic capa-

---

[3] In the sense of "mixed manning," NATO has no integrated *forces;* the only mixed-manned organizations are *headquarters*—SHAPE, the Major Subordinate Commands (Allied Forces Northern Region, Allied Forces Central Region, Allied Forces Mediterranean, and Allied Forces Southern Region), the Army Groups (e.g., Central Army Group), and the Allied Tactical Air Forces. NATO uses the term integrated air defense," but this is not a mixed-manned force; each of its operational components is made up of organizations which are all of one nationality, and only the *command* is "integrated" since it is exercised through headquarters in the alliance chain of command which are themselves internationally staffed.

bilities of the member countries." The TCC in three months prepared "the first comprehensive review of how the resources of the member countries under peacetime conditions can best be employed in the interest of common security." Subsequently, the annual review and planning became one of the most important functions of NATO's Secretariat.

In political affairs NATO's secretary general emerged as an official of major importance. Lord Ismay was appointed vice chairman of the Council and secretary general of NATO in April 1952. He was succeeded in the spring of 1957 by a dynamic statesmen, Paul-Henri Spaak of Belgium. Until 1957 ministerial Council sessions, usually two a year, were under a chairmanship rotating among the foreign ministers of member countries. In accord with the Council's decision in December 1956, the secretary general has become the presiding officer at all Council meetings, including ministerial sessions, and the rotating chairmanship of the foreign ministers has served mainly for ceremonial functions. The secretary general, his deputy, and other high officials of the Secretariat take a more important political role than international civil servants usually do in international organizations. The secretaries general of NATO represented continuity, strengthened the Alliance, and supported cooperative policy in the North Atlantic area. This trend has not changed since the resignation of Secretary Spaak on January 1, 1961. His distinguished successors, Dirk U. Stikker (1961-1964) and Manlio Brosio (1964-   ) vigorously continued established NATO policies.[4] All member states have appointed representatives to NATO. These representatives formed a special diplomatic body in Paris, in addition to the group of diplomats accredited to the French government and to OECD.

Germany's admission to NATO was made possible by the Paris agreements, signed in October 1954, which transformed the Brussels Treaty into the Western European Union (WEU). The German Federal Republic and Italy acceded to the modified Treaty. In view of these agreements France, the United Kingdom, and the United States terminated the occupation regime in the Federal Republic of Germany, and with some restriction recognized the Bonn Republic as a sovereign state. A Consultative Assembly,[5] a Council, and an Agency for the Control of Armaments are the organs of WEU. Britain and the United States pledged to maintain military forces on the Continent of Europe.

---

[4] Several secretaries general published memoirs and reports about NATO problems. See Lord Ismay, *NATO, the First Five Years, 1949-1954* (NATO publication); Lord Ismay's "Report to the Ministerial Meeting of the North Atlantic Council at Bonn, May, 1957," *NATO Letter*, V (June 1957); *The Memoirs of General Lord Ismay* (New York: The Viking Press, 1960); Paul-Henri Spaak, *Why NATO* (Baltimore: Penguin Books, 1959); Dirk U. Stikker, *op. cit.*

[5] See above, p. 125.

NATO's strategy became the "shield and sword" concept, which meant that in a major conflict the shield forces would resist Soviet aggression in Europe while the United States and British strategic air forces and missiles would retaliate against the Soviet Union.[6]

Despite development of NATO's military strength, coordination of NATO action must come in each instance through diplomatic negotiation. The Council is a permanent diplomatic conference without supranational power. Its members have the spirit of cooperation, but they must consider public opinion and domestic conditions much more than do representatives of dictatorships. NATO's structure supposes an agreement in the North Atlantic Council without which no directives can go to the military commanders. Diplomatic machinery is the cornerstone of the Western alliance. General Norstad put the problem in the following way:

> Our present strategy, influenced as it must be by the hopes and the needs of 15 nations, is inevitably one of compromise. This has certainly given us a useful start. But for the Alliance to have continuing life and meaning, it needs an increasing authority. Action to pass to the Alliance greater control over atomic weapons and subjecting their use more directly to the collective will, if politically feasible, could be a great new step.[7]

Growth of Consultative Diplomacy

Even the strongest NATO arsenal would be of doubtful value if policy-making were not in harmony with contemporary requirements. In view of the political nature of the NATO Alliance, responsibility for decision and

---

[6] For the growth of NATO's military organization and strategic problems, see *The NATO Handbook* (Paris: North Atlantic Treaty Organization Information Service, 1965); *NATO: Facts About the North Atlantic Treaty Organization* (Paris: NATO Information Service, 1965); Ben T. Moore, *NATO and the Future of Europe* (New York: Harper & Row, Publishers, Inc., 1958); Klaus Knorr, ed., *NATO and American Security* (Princeton: Princeton University Press, 1959); M. Margaret Ball, *NATO and the European Union Movement* (London: Stevens, 1959); Robert Endicott Osgood, *NATO: The Entangling Alliance* (Chicago: University of Chicago Press, 1962); Alastair Buchan, *NATO in the 1960's* (New York: Frederick A. Praeger, 1963); Alastair Buchan and Philip Windsor, *Arms and Stability in Europe* (London: Chatto & Windus, Ltd., 1963); Robert Kleiman, *Atlantic Crisis: American Diplomacy Confronts a Resurgent Europe* (New York: W. W. Norton & Company, Inc., 1964); Ronald Steel, *The End of Alliance* (New York: The Viking Press, 1964); Raymond Aron, *The Great Debate* (Garden City, N.Y.: Doubleday and Co., Inc., 1965); F. W. Mulley, *The Politics of Western Defense* (New York: Frederick A. Praeger, 1962); Henry A. Kissinger, *The Troubled Partnership* (New York: McGraw-Hill Book Co., 1965); Edgar S. Furniss, Jr., ed., *The Western Alliance, Its Status and Prospects* (Columbus: Ohio State University Press, 1965); Timothy W. Stanley, *NATO in Transition: The Future of the Atlantic Alliance* (New York: Frederick A. Praeger, 1965). Harold Van B. Cleveland, *The Atlantic Idea and its European Rivals* (New York: McGraw-Hill Book Co., 1966).

[7] *NATO Letter,* VIII (January 1960), 10.

action rests on national governments, and thus the efficiency of inter-allied diplomacy is of utmost importance.

One of the most significant developments in NATO is the institutionalization of multilateral consultation in the Council, where international political problems are collectively discussed. Artice 4 of the North Atlantic Treaty provided for consultation of member states "whenever, in the opinion of any of them, the territorial integrity, political independence or security of any of the Parties is threatened." Consultation was used only sporadically during the first five years of NATO, but events in 1955, and particularly the Suez crisis in 1956, gave impetus to consultation. The Berlin Conference in 1955 and both Geneva conferences have followed preparatory meetings of the North Atlantic Council at which delegates of the fifteen NATO members discussed problems of international politics relevant to negotiation with the Soviet Union. France, Britain, and the United States had no mandate to negotiate agreements with the USSR in the name of other NATO countries. They consulted the other NATO countries before negotiating with the Russians. The NATO Council has become an instrument for continuous consultation. It should be noted, parenthetically, that there is a sharp difference between the procedure and attitudes in consultation, and that in formal negotiation aiming at specific agreements.

At NATO consultation has become a daily process in which the skill of diplomats sometimes may be more important than the power of their respective countries. This is one of the reasons why most states have been represented in the Council by outstanding plenipotentiaries. The quality of representation has assured high standards in NATO discussions, and Council members clearly and directly have transmitted and interpreted NATO policies for their governments. If unity exists, an exchange of information and opinion by experienced representatives may help even the strongest power. This method is more practical than bilateral consultation. Discussion in NATO often illuminates events and constitutes a mutual educative process of the highest order.

The Council meets at least once a week, at which time the secretary general submits topics for discussion. The following week, representatives of the member governments may take positions. On the Council's instruction the Political Affairs Division of the Secretariat sometimes prepares background papers on political problems to be discussed in the Council. These papers go to delegations of member countries and to the Committee of Political Advisors where deputy heads usually represent the delegation. This Committee also performs tasks in connection with exchange of information and views in NATO and the harmonization and coordination of

NATO policies; often the NATO Council instructs the Political Committee to discuss problems with a view to harmony or coordination. Preparatory work by the Political Affairs Division of the Secretariat and by the NATO Committee of Political Advisors is of importance because it is desirable that the outline of the position acceptable to fifteen member countries be worked out before Council meetings. Any ambassador accredited to NATO may ask for a special meeting restricted to heads of missions. The intimate character of such conferences is in sharp contrast with regular Council meetings in which a large number of specialists participate.

Careful preparation helps the task of the Council, which becomes an instrument for unity. The following are categories for consultation:

First—Relations between the NATO area and the Soviet Union. The Soviet threat to all NATO members is the primary reason for the alliance.

Second—Advancement of the ends of NATO. This category pertains to peaceful settlement of any international dispute involving NATO members (Article 1), and particularly to application of Article 2 for "the further development of peaceful and friendly international relations by strengthening their free institutions, by bringing about a better understanding of the principles upon which these institutions are founded, and by promoting conditions of stability and well-being."

Examples of conflicts between member states are the Icelandic territorial sea and fishery controversy and the case of Cyprus. The Cyprus settlement of 1960 was not negotiated in NATO but was facilitated by NATO's efforts at conciliation. Even during the most violent periods of the civil war in Cyprus, representatives of Greece and Turkey remained on speaking terms in the Council and, with help of the secretary general, were working for a settlement. In such delicate matters the Council is often able to explore settlement through consultation. Nevertheless, NATO's failure to deal effectively with the Cyprus conflict was more important than what it did to help conciliation. When emotions dominate a situation, consultation or any other reasonable procedure is difficult. The persisting Cyprus conflict is an example of such a predicament. Although Cyprus has been an independent state since 1960, it is not a member of NATO; the conflict remains a disagreement between Greece and Turkey. The problem is complicated by the fact that a third NATO country, Britain, retains two military bases in Cyprus.

The conflict between Britain and Iceland concerning the limits of Icelandic territorial waters also displayed a weakness of NATO diplomacy, which arises whenever member states in dispute are unwilling to accept a reasonable settlement. The United Kingdom accepted a solution worked out by NATO in 1958, which would have satisfied materially all legitimate Icelandic interests. But the Icelandic government could not compromise because of the country's delicate internal political balance;[8] it demanded *de jure* recognition of the twelve-mile limit. Eventually, in an agreement signed in February 1961, Britain conceded almost all Icelandic demands. Iceland's defiance of a powerful ally and her rejection of NATO's recommendation proved her independence.

Third—If consultation is valuable for advancing NATO's purposes within its own sphere, it has increasing importance outside NATO's jurisdiction. The Soviet threat has assumed a worldwide character, and it is difficult to draw a line between areas within and outside NATO's jurisdiction. Several NATO members have interests in the Far East, Middle East, Africa, and other areas beyond NATO's jurisdiction, and a growing category of consultations relates to exchange of information and views on developments outside of NATO.

Consultation has worked out a united Western proposal in disarmament. Indeed, disarmament may be considered within the sphere of NATO, because it is so closely connected with the whole defense strategy with respect to the USSR. Throughout the London negotiations between the USSR and the Western Four in the summer of 1957, an informal liaison was maintained with the NATO Council in Paris. Simultaneous negotiation in London and Paris made possible the united Western proposal at the Disarmament Conference in London in August of that year. This united Western position was supported not only by Western European countries, but also in the 12th General Assembly of the United Nations by twenty-four nations which sponsored a resolution endorsing the Western proposals. In the final vote fifty-seven states accepted the resolution, with only the Soviet bloc voting against it.[9] Arrival at common policy in such a complicated field as disarmament is a striking example of fruitful consultation among NATO powers.

Favorable trends in NATO consultation have occasionally balanced serious setbacks. Consultation was in full operation in 1956 when the second half of the year witnessed a hardening of the cold war caused by the Polish upheaval, the Hungarian revolution, and the secretly prepared Anglo-French action in Suez. The Suez affair was a case which should have been a direct concern of NATO, but there was no consultation. Lack of cooperation was the result of political mistakes and of mutual lack of confidence. This in-

[8] Iceland had a coalition government which included two communist cabinet ministers.

[9] *Disarmament: The Intensified Effort 1955-58* (Washington: Department of State, 1958), p. 57.

cident could have threatened the very existence of NATO. Nothing proved better the vitality of NATO than the fact that the Suez crisis strengthened the organization. An important result of the unilateral Anglo-French action and the hostile American response, as well as of the Soviet intervention in Hungary, was a general realization of the need for Western unity. Britain and the continental countries showed remarkable solidarity, although many European states were not sympathetic with the Anglo-French action at Suez.

Amidst the dramatic events in 1956, NATO strengthened its multilateral diplomacy. The Committee of Three on Non-Military Cooperation in NATO, set up in May "to advise the Council on ways to improve and extend NATO cooperation in non-military fields and to develop greater unity within the Atlantic Community," consisted of three foreign ministers—Lester B. Pearson of Canada, Gaetano Martino of Italy, and Halvard Lange of Norway. The committee sent out a questionnaire to each NATO member, and analysis of replies preceded consultation with member states. The draft of the report made up by the committee was re-examined in November 1956 in light of the preceding events. The final text was approved at the Ministerial Council Meeting in December 1956. The report was a program both for cooperation in political, economic, cultural, and information fields and for the organization and functioning of NATO: "An Alliance in which the members ignore each other's interests or engage in political or economic conflict, or harbor suspicions of each other, cannot be effective either for deterrence or defense. Recent experience makes this clearer than ever before." The report emphasized "a pressing requirement for all members to make consultation in NATO an integral part of the making of national policy." To have effective political consultation, members "should inform the Council of any development which significantly affects the Alliance." At their annual spring meeting the NATO foreign ministers "should make an appraisal of the political progress of the Alliance and consider the lines along which it should advance." The secretary general should submit an annual report as a basis for discussion among the foreign ministers. Peaceful settlement of disputes within NATO before resorting to any other international agency was recommended. The secretary general was empowered "to offer his good offices informally at any time to the parties in dispute, and with their consent to initiate or facilitate procedures of inquiry, mediation, conciliation, or arbitration." The Three Wise Men of 1956 emphasized:

It has also become increasingly realized since the Treaty was signed that security is today far more than a military matter. The strengthening of political consultation and economic co-operation, the development of resources, progress in education and public understanding, all these can be as important, or even more important, for the protection of the security of a nation, or an alliance, as the building of a battleship or the equipping of an army.

If consultation is not new, governments have never before used it so extensively and regularly. Views were exchanged on such matters as the Berlin crisis and reunification of Germany, negotiation at the summit, suspension of nuclear tests, and establishment of zones of inspection to prevent surprise attack. In harmony with this cooperation, in the spring of 1958 the United States disclosed to the Council its policies concerning Taiwan and the Chinese offshore islands. In a similar way Britain and the United States discussed the 1958 Middle Eastern situation in the Council, and made clear that under certain circumstances they would respond with military assistance to the request of friendly governments endangered by subversion and aggression. At that time the United States had received a request from President Camille Chamoun of Lebanon who, explaining that his regime was threatened by external aggression, asked for support. The American delegate pointed out in the NATO Council that the United States would like to avoid military intervention in Lebanon but that events might make it necessary. When a coup took place in Iraq there was no time for another consultation, and President Eisenhower simply ordered Marines to land in Lebanon. Political circles in some NATO countries, France and Turkey in particular, resented the fact that a second consultation did not take place before intervention.

From the point of view of results, the following can be said about NATO consultations:

First—Consultation is successful when a meeting of minds is possible.

Second—It may well be that consultation will not produce an agreement and some NATO members may decide to follow different courses. Such consultation would be unsuccessful even though it at least would clarify attitudes. Unsuccessful consultation took place in July 1958 when the United States and Britain accepted and France opposed a summit meeting within the United Nations Security Council. The NATO Council failed to reconcile differing Allied views, and President de Gaulle, in his separate letter to Khrushchev, stated that he preferred a summit conference at Geneva to a special session of the United Nations on the Middle East. Difference of policy is not necessarily harmful, and there are areas in which the unity of NATO members is not essential. But mutual understanding of the controverted issues is important. It would not be wise for NATO states to form a bloc in the United Nations. It may be debatable whether in some cases a uniform NATO policy is desirable. It has been assumed that the spirit of cooperation resulting from exchange of ideas in the NATO Council promotes common policies even without binding agreements.

Third—Consultation is most unsatisfactory when some member states announce their policies in the Council and the majority of the ambassadors do not react—as was the case in the summer of 1958 when Britain and the United States declared their intentions concerning conflicts in the Middle and Far East. Small powers have a reasonable explanation for their reserved attitude. Parliaments and the public in some small countries are not always interested in a conflict outside NATO's proper area and most of them are unwilling to take a position in cases outside NATO's jurisdiction. They have little information through their own channels on Far Eastern and other non-NATO problems and they naturally are reluctant to express an opinion.

Secretary General Spaak gave a different view of the responsibilities of small NATO states in matters outside NATO's immediate area. Pointing out in a speech before the Conference of NATO Parliamentarians in November 1958 that several countries remained silent regarding the Anglo-American statement of policy in Middle Eastern affairs, he gave the following interpretation of consultation:

> From the moment when we claim that we can be consulted because we know that a conflict breaking out in the Middle East could have direct repercussions on our own situation, we are committed; from the moment when we call for consultations and still more take part in them, that is, give our views, then our responsibility begins. . . .[10]

This far-reaching interpretation of "responsibility through consultation" is not acceptable to most small powers. Even Spaak pointed out that he did not know whether diplomatic silence in the Council meant yes or no.

Can NATO achieve a united policy in important questions beyond the treaty area? That smaller countries prefer not to say anything in discussion of such problems is due to the fact that they either do not have the necessary information or else have no opinion as to how far NATO action in outside matters should go. Underlying their attitude is reluctance to extend their NATO commitments outside the treaty area, even by implication.

If NATO consultation is a new method of collective diplomacy, it is not surprising that some aspects of it are unclear. When great powers such as the United States and Britain submit important diplomatic notes to the NATO Council and discuss foreign political problems with representatives of small powers we have an example of a revolution in diplomacy. Spaak has commented:

> The only word I can find to describe this new picture is "moving," when we see . . . that President Eisenhower does not write to M. Bulganin or to M. Khrushchev without making sure that his letter is approved by the head of the Government or by the Foreign Minister of the smallest country in the Alliance.[11]

It is true that disparity in economic and military power, and in world responsibilities, is a source of difficulty in consultation. There are, moreover, special difficulties for the United States. A superpower has a certain loneliness. In the case of the Cuban missile crisis in 1962, President Kennedy informed some of the major NATO powers of his decision and notified the NATO Council of what the United States was doing, and the Council approved it, although there was no genuine NATO consultation. The strongest power in NATO has world problems of a different nature than European states. Power or lack of power contributes to different responsibilities and points of view. NATO consultation may facilitate the solution of conflicts, but it cannot eliminate the substantial differences that originate in varying ideas of the Soviet threat and of the best Western responses. Domestic political considerations, national interests, and diverse approaches to political problems may cause friction.

Nevertheless, institutionalization of consultation in NATO has not created common Western policies in some fundamental issues, nor could it hinder the increasing disarray of the Western Alliance. The experience of a decade had demonstrated that some important questions have not been discussed in the NATO Council. France did not consult her NATO partners in connection with Algeria or the fundamental change in her policy toward China and toward NATO. The Anglo-French Suez action and President Kennedy's ultimatum to the USSR during the Cuban missile crisis were not discussed in the Council. The Johnson administration did not inform, let alone consult, NATO before sending troops to Santo Domingo in 1965. Even if we disregard the handling of some vital issues, the enthusiastic expectations expressed so eloquently by Secretary Spaak in 1958 have not been justified. The Council meetings have become similar to regular conferences where diplomats express opinion on the basis of instruction. Under these conditions the weekly Council meeting is evermore restricted to routine exchange of information.

[11] *Ibid.*, pp. 7-8.

Although consultation has been in force for more than a decade, the Western alliance system seems to divide on several major issues in world politics. During the dangerous years of the cold war the situation was more simple. NATO members cooperated against the common threat, and the Soviet advance was stopped in Europe. NATO's original purpose was accomplished. This success has become in a sense a source of weakness, because NATO members have no treaty obligation to take a stand, let alone to act, outside the territorial scope of the Alliance. Although the Report of the "Three Wise Men" of 1956 emphasized that the interests of NATO states "are not confined to the area covered by the Treaty," a NATO policy concerning territorial possessions of NATO states in Asia and Africa has not been possible. China has become another dividing factor because it represents a different threat to the United States than to European countries. Hence also the reserved attitude of NATO countries in connection with United States involvements in Southern Asia.

Consultation has remained important within NATO, and it can develop and diversify according to changing world conditions. One of the desirable improvements could be institutionalization of some new methods, such as bimonthly ministerial meetings and regular conferences of high officials with decision-making power at home. Meetings of specialists in charge of areas and meetings of undersecretaries and assistant secretaries have proved fruitful in recent years. In early 1965 a meeting on the foreign minister and undersecretary level discussed the Far Eastern situation and related matters. Besides top-level meetings, there are meetings of regional specialists from foreign offices. There is a sense of participation in these groups. Not only do such conferences make possible exchange of opinions, but participants have the benefit of factual information which they would not otherwise obtain.

NATO consultation has been supplemented by the Atlantic Policy Advisory Group. Each member state appoints one representative—usually the head of the policy planning staff or another high official from the foreign ministry. The group meets twice a year under chairmanship of the head of NATO's Political Affairs Division. At the outset representatives of small states manifested a reserved attitude, but more recently they have become interested because of the entirely free argument in these meetings. Such an uninhibited discussion enables small states to understand the motives and actions of great powers. The Advisory Group discusses policy options and alternatives. Such debates have a much greater effect on policy formation than does the mere explanation of current policies—even if the explanations are followed by some discussions. In traditional diplomacy, policy alternatives were considered tabu, not to be revealed to, let alone discussed with, representatives of other countries. These discussions seem to provide a sense of community spirit among NATO members. Certainly, they are a school of highest quality for diplomats of the Atlantic nations.

TEN

NATO's Crisis
and Europe's Future

President de Gaulle announced on September 9, 1965, that after the year 1969 France no longer would accept an integrated North Atlantic military defense system. He recognized that in many areas France had "the best reasons for associating with others," but that she nevertheless must retain her self-determination:

so long as the solidarity of the Western peoples appears to us necessary for the eventual defense of Europe, our country will remain the ally of her allies but, upon the expiration of the commitments formerly taken—that is, in 1969 by the latest—the subordination known as "integration" which is provided for by NATO and which hands our fate over to foreign authority shall cease, as far as we are concerned.

De Gaulle's pronouncement did not come as a surprise, since for the last few years he and his advisers privately had expressed similar opinions. His statement was the overture to French diplomatic action. At a press conference of February 21, 1966, de Gaulle told his audience that France would "modify successively the measures currently practiced" before the right of denunciation of the North Atlantic Treaty will come into effect on April 4, 1969.

It means re-establishing a normal situation of sovereignty, so that everything French, including soil, sky, sea and forces, and any foreign element in France will in the future be under French command alone.

De Gaulle warned of the danger of a conflagration resulting from American engagements in other continents. He said that in that case

Europe—whose strategy is, within NATO, that of America—would be automatically involved in the struggle, even when it would not have so desired. It would be so for France, if the intermeshing of her territory, of her communications, of certain of her forces, of several of her air bases, of some of her ports with the military system under American command were to continue much longer.

Subsequent political steps were prepared in the best tradition of French diplomacy. For maximum effect the schedule was coordinated with de Gaulle's visit to the Soviet Union.[1] A spectacular separation from NATO's integrated structure strengthened his position with the Kremlin.

In handwritten letters of March 7, 1966 President de Gaulle informed President Johnson, Chancellor Erhard, and the British and Italian Prime Ministers of the new turn of French foreign policy. These letters contained assurance that unless events changed the facts directing East-West relations, France would, "in 1969 and beyond, be determined, as today, to fight on the side of her Allies in the event that one of them should be the object of an *unprovoked aggression*" (Italics mine). With the expression "unprovoked aggression," France introduced a new terminology in NATO. Since the days of the League of Nations many vain attempts have been made to define aggression. Article 5 of the North Atlantic Treaty made individual or collective self-defense dependent on an "armed attack," easily recognizable. Irrespective of the fact that in the missile age there might be no time to ascertain the nature of aggression, the French government could opt in each case for cooperation with NATO or neutrality by the simple definition of the "provoked" or "unprovoked" nature of an aggression for which no objective criteria exist.

In March 1966 the French Government in an *aide-mémoire* sent to the other fourteen NATO governments explained that the threat to Europe that had led to the Atlantic Treaty no longer had the same menacing character; France had atomic weapons, "the very nature of which precludes her integration"; American nuclear monopoly was replaced by a nuclear balance between the Soviet Union and the United States—a fact which transformed the conditions of Western defense; finally, Europe no longer was a center of international crises—most crises occurred in Asia, where the majority of NATO countries were not involved. The memorandum stated that the French government would have been happy to modify NATO arrangements by common agreement but it was obvious that negotiations would fail, "since all France's partners either appear to be, or say that they

[1] See above, p. 55.

are, in favor of maintaining the *'status quo,'* if not of reinforcing every-thing which France henceforth considers unacceptable." In view of these circumstances France announced her request for the withdrawal from French soil of all United States and Canadian military bases as well as of SHAPE. She also announced a decision to withdraw from the integrated allied defense organization the two divisions and two air squadrons sta-tioned in West Germany. Simultaneously, with rejection of a permanent peacetime defense system, the French government expressed willingness to discuss contingency plans—that is, circumstances in which military facilities on French territory could be put at disposal of the United States "in the event of a conflict in which both countries would participate by virtue of the Atlantic Alliance."

The fourteen NATO partners on March 18 issued a short declaration of loyalty toward an "integrated and interdependent military organization" of NATO and expressed their conviction that no system of bilateral arrange-ments could substitute for it:

> The North Atlantic Treaty and the organization are not merely instru-ments of the common defense. They meet a common political need and reflect the readiness and determination of the member countries of the North Atlantic Community to consult and act together wherever possible in the safeguard of their freedom and security and in the furtherance of inter-national peace, progress and prosperity.

President Johnson's reply to President de Gaulle (March 23, 1966) pointed out that the Alliance reflected two important propositions. The first was that if war should come to the Atlantic area the Allies must fight together—and fight effectively. The second was that if the Allies acted together for the common interest during peace, war would not come. The President expressed his respect for France's pledge to fight beside her Allies if any NATO member should suffer unprovoked aggression, but thought that more was needed to achieve deterrence. He was puzzled by de Gaulle's view that the presence of allied military forces on French soil impaired the sovereignty of France since these forces had been there at French invitation to insure the security of France and her allies. In the President's view, "Readiness to fight instantly under agreed plans and procedures, worked out and practiced in peacetime," added immeasurably to NATO's strength. He referred to the danger of relying in crisis on inde-pendent action by separate forces "in accordance with national plans, only loosely coordinated with joint forces and plans."

After these skirmishes, the unyielding French *aide-mémoire* of March 29 laid down the deadlines to liberate France from institutional links with NATO. The note indicated that French military personnel would be withdrawn from integrated military command by July 1, 1966, and from the NATO Defense College by July 23. July 1 was the date for withdrawal from NATO command of the two French divisions stationed in West Germany. The agreements under which the alliance's military headquarters were housed in France were denounced, with completion of the transfer of the headquarters by April 1, 1967. The French Government set this short deadline for removal of American Military headquarters and installations from France.

Contrary to diplomatic traditions between friendly countries, the *aide-mémoire* disregarded legal niceties in connection with the bilateral agreements France had concluded with the United States and Canada. Four of the agreements with the United States concerned air bases, an air depot, a NATO pipeline, and the headquarters near Paris. These treaties could not be terminated prior to 1969 except by "mutual consent." A fifth agreement, concerning communications and army depots, provided for a two-year denunciation period.

The French argued that these agreements would no longer apply in view of decisions taken by the French government regarding its nonparticipation in NATO's integrated structure. In other words, the unilateral French action created a new situation which was used to void the treaties before their expiration, although the treaties did not have a clause for unilateral renunciation.

In harmony with this timetable, the French military personnel and the two divisions stationed in Germany were withdrawn from NATO command, the French representative was withdrawn from the tripartite Standing Group, and France stopped paying its share of NATO's military expenses, except for certain organs and functions in which she wished to participate.

Allied military bases, headquarters, and other evicted NATO organs, in turn, left France. SHAPE was relocated to Casteau in Belgium, the NATO Defense College to Rome, and the NATO Council decided to move to Brussels. Although the French procedure was most unusual and caused great harm, inconvenience, and expenditure, the Allies decided to avoid recrimination and made changes within NATO as smoothly as possible.

Modification of the NATO Treaty was not necessary to meet the French demands because the huge military organization was established on the basis of inter-Allied decisions. Article 9 of the Treaty authorized the NATO Council to "set up such subsidiary bodies as may be necessary." With unanimous consent and the cooperation of all member states, NATO had developed a military and diplomatic organization, communication network, infrastructure installations, and logistic systems.[2]

Another point worth noting is that the North Atlantic Treaty will not expire in 1969, as is sometimes asserted, for only the right of denunciation of the Treaty will come into effect at that time. After 1969 the NATO Treaty could continue, with or without organizational changes; the permanent organization could be eliminated, in which case NATO would become a conventional alliance; finally, the treaty could be amended in a variety of ways. Under Article 12 each member state has had, since 1959, the right to initiate amendment of the Treaty but none has insisted on doing so. Reminiscent of the situation in 1917-1918, NATO could consist of two groups: Allied and Associated powers. During World War I the United States was an Associated power, because "no entanglement" and "no alliance" was the American tradition. In 1917-1918 this nomenclature was not much more than a distinction without a difference. In practice, the United States had been a full-fledged member of the Western Alliance and President Wilson played a leading role at the Peace Conference. But in NATO the difference between allied and associated status could be important in organizational matters. Some NATO powers might desire to enlarge the integrated commands, while others might take a more reserved position. Even now great flexibility exists. Iceland does not have an army; the Danish and Norwegian armies do not participate in training in the use of atomic weapons; the bulk of the Portuguese army is in Africa.

Existence of two categories of states in NATO is a *pis aller,* but a clear situation is better than sabotage from within by a sulking partner. Most NATO countries prefer a full-fledged status, with integrated command. France might become a sort of associated member without participating in any commands, as might other nations. As NATO would remain an alliance in any case, in a crisis member states in both categories would have to agree on principles of common defense and on other duties. Although the role of the United States should not be that of an insurance company which gives full coverage to members who refuse to pay premiums, in practice this is the case. The American atomic umbrella over Europe and the American troops in Germany automatically defend France, irrespective of the vagaries of French politics.

Whether or not we accept the "Allied and Associated" terminology,

---

[2] NATO Common Infrastructure Installations (airfields, communication systems, radar installations, naval facilities, missile sites, headquarters and training installations, etc.) are financed collectively by NATO member countries under the terms of various cost-sharing agreements. Such NATO installations set up on a national territory can be used by the forces of any other member country. Since 1951 the North Atlantic Council approved Common Infrastructure "slices" amounting to a total of about $4 billion.

de Gaulle created for France a special status in NATO. He disassociated France from many NATO decisions, made with French participation if not upon French initiative. Gaullist policies increasingly have been harmful to inter-Allied interests. Since 1958 France has refused to cooperate in many important NATO policies and in world affairs has been taking anti-American attitudes,[3] with almost irrational eagerness, except during the Cuban missile crisis. One may wonder about French reactions if American leaders had expressed strong anti-French views during the colonial wars in Indo-China and Algeria. Although geography and traditions would make desirable French leadership in Atlantic affairs, Gaullist France apparently decided on a different course.

None of the alliance's members supports the French demand to abolish NATO's integrated structure. They believe that the transformation of NATO into a simple alliance would be a great step backward, politically and militarily. Return to "normal alliances" woud be an excellent idea if accompanied by a return to "normal times," including abolition of missiles, thermonuclear weapons, totalitarian dictatorships, and ideological factors in world politics.

Organizational changes in NATO doubtless are necessary; at the least, some major criticisms concerning NATO's present structure deserve examination. In view of complaints because of lack of close relations and satisfactory communication between the Military Committee and Standing Group in Washington, on the one hand, and the Atlantic Council on the other, the transfer of the two military establishments from Washington to the vicinity of the Atlantic Council could improve the relations between NATO's major diplomatic and military organs.

Viewed from a broader perspective, NATO could remain a regional defense organization, or it could be transformed, through amendments, into an organization dealing with worldwide problems. It would be possible to modify the NATO Treaty (Articles 4, 5, and 6) so as to universalize NATO obligations. This would mean that a threat to any NATO member in any part of the world, under any conditions, would be NATO's business. If a universalization of NATO's functions and obligations might meet opposition from several states, NATO could have two categories of members: those with general and others with limited interests and obligations.

A more sweeping solution would be to leave NATO's regional character unchanged, and to establish a separate organization of free nations to deal with major world political problems in other parts of the world. Still, al-

---

[3] Dirk U. Stikker, former Secretary General of NATO enumerated some actions and inactions characteristic of French noncooperation between 1958 and 1964. *Men of Responsibility*, pp. 301-2.

though a worldwide Western cooperation on basic issues is necessary, the policy of some major Western powers does not seem to be moving in this direction.

One possible long-range solution would be establishment of NATO as an independent nuclear power, with the British and French atomic forces and a possible American contribution under international control. But whether such a collective force should be under NATO or a Western European Political Authority depends on future developments. Alternatively, NATO could be reorganized on the basis of the ellipses theory—with two centers, one in Washington, the other in Europe. According to this plan, the Political Authority of a European Union—in addition to the American President—would have power of decision in European atomic matters.

Under certain conditions the creation of a European Political Authority would help solve long-range problems between the United States and European members of the Alliance. If Europe should unite politically, the French *force de frappe* and the British atomic weapons could become the nucleus of an integrated European Army, organized possibly within NATO or the Western European Union. NATO's nuclear forces would have American and Western European components, and the United States probably would help strengthen the European atomic deterrent.

Such proposals for a major reorganization of the Western Alliance, no matter how desirable, may not be feasible in the foreseeable future. It is necessary to look at immediate exigencies. A European Political Authority is far from a reality. There is no indication of French eagerness to hand over to a European collective body even part of her control of the *force de frappe.* President de Gaulle demands for Europe equality with the United States and he speaks of a "European Europe" which in his semantics means a Europe without Americans and under French leadership. He is willing to lead Europe as head of a country with some atomic capability, but European members of NATO do not seem anxious to replace American commitments, and particularly the presence of American troops in Europe.

For the United States it might be convenient to deal with a French partner who is recognized as their spokesman, at least informally, by Western European countries. But though de Gaulle likes to speak as defender of Europe's interests, not one European country outside France is willing to accept him as Europe's representative. It is one thing for the United States to welcome a European arrangement which would make it possible for a Frenchman to represent Europe, but quite another to impose French leadership on European states.

In France and in some other European countries apprehensions stem from changing strategies connected with rapid transformation of weapons systems. Some Europeans fear that the United States would refuse to authorize a nuclear response as soon as the European governments think it necessary. Debate between the advocates of "massive retaliation" and of "graduated response" is part of the policy problem involved. In reality the issue raised by some Europeans is not a greater European voice in planning or policy, but, to put it bluntly, a European ability to insure the use of nuclear weapons despite United States refusal. This European anxiety could be dispelled only by giving Western Europe the power to override a United States veto on the use of nuclear weapons, or by the creation of an autonomous, European-controlled nuclear force, powerful enough to meet what they view as the requirements of deterrence. The issue involved is a question of confidence which originates in the difference between American and some European views with respect to nuclear strategy. There is, however, a preliminary difficulty in this complex problem. Without a European Political Authority, the United States does not have a partner with whom to settle the pertinent delicate questions. Views expressed by European allies are far from unanimous.

Under prevailing international conditions, a single nuclear deterrent force within NATO seems more realistic than speculation about cooperation between a nonexistent European Political Authority and the United States. One of the difficulties between the United States and some of its European allies originates in different approaches to strategic thinking. While American strategy distinguishes between ability to repel an attack and strict punishment, European critics of American strategy think primarily of punishment when they discuss deterrence. A reasonable remedy seems to be the establishment of political machinery to allow European countries more participation in the early stage of policy determination concerning the use of nuclear weapons.

In the past American diplomacy tried a different approach. Some American policy-makers thought that common ownership and management of a mixed-manned force could lead toward a common Atlantic nuclear policy and eventually to an Atlantic nuclear community. Only Germany welcomed the idea of a NATO nuclear fleet, but even German ambitions were deflated in view of de Gaulle's opposition. Eventually the Multilateral Force and the British Atlantic Force became dead issues.

Most European statesmen recognize that defense in NATO must have central organization and that the ultimate decision—to push the button in a nuclear war—rests for the time being with the President of the United States. To avoid the necessity of such a decision is the purpose of NATO. In the atomic age the achievement of the NATO powers has been to contain

Soviet expansion in Europe without war. Military alliances do not survive the disappearance of the *casus foederis,* the reason of the alliance, and some people nurture the illusion that the common danger no longer threatens. This wishful thinking is strange in view of the increasing Soviet military preparation and especially the more than 700 medium and intermediate-range ballistic missiles trained on targets in Western Europe from Soviet bases.

In my opinion, an agreement on policies among leading NATO powers is more important than formal revision of the Treaty or organizational changes. Important differences in policies and approaches have developed within the Alliance between the United States and nonatomic powers as well as between the United States and powers with limited atomic capabilities. Washington proposed to mitigate these differences by granting members of the other groups broader participation in atomic planning and training through the Multilateral Nuclear Force, but the fate of the MLF is a symbol of the disarray within the Alliance which has not adapted its role to changing conditions. Without the agreement of leading NATO powers on some major purposes in world politics, NATO, necessary as it is, cannot attain its objectives. It is a good idea to follow different policies toward different communist states, but in view of the variety of methods for this purpose, agreement is needed on some basic aspects of policies.

Creation of new institutions or organizational changes are not substitutes for agreement on policies; establishment of new institutions would transfer policy disagreements to different spheres. If NATO members are unable to reach agreement on fundamental policies in world affairs and on the means for achieving them, the Alliance cannot survive, irrespective of organizational perfection. Institutional changes might camouflage conflicting policies for a while, but they are not a cure-all for them. Of course, agreements would be needed only in connection with a few fundamental issues. Diversity in approaches and policy differences, if kept within limits, are not weaknesses; they may even add to the flexibility of a free association of nations.

General de Gaulle attempted to solve a genuine problem when, in a letter of September 17, 1958, to President Eisenhower and Prime Minister Harold Macmillan, he proposed an American-French-British directorate to make joint strategy decisions on political questions affecting world security and to work out strategic plans of action, notably with regard to nuclear weapons. The United States and Britain could not accept the proposal for several reasons. President Eisenhower pointed out in his reply of October 20 that the established "procedures for organizing the defense of the free world clearly require the willing cooperation of many other nations, both within and outside NATO." He pointed out that

We cannot afford to adopt any system which would give to our other allies, or other free world countries, the impression that basic decisions affecting their own vital interests are being made without their participation.

Some unworkable features notwithstanding, de Gaulle's idea was a sound one and NATO accepted it in due course, but without French participation. After several preliminary steps, fourteen NATO Ministers met as the Defense Planning Committee on December 14, 1966, and agreed to establish in NATO two permanent bodies for nuclear planning. The first is the Nuclear Defense Affairs Committee (NDAC). Its primary responsibility is to propose general policy concerning all aspects of nuclear defense. This strategy committee is open to all members of the Alliance and presently twelve nations are represented in it. Under NDAC a smaller committee, known as the Nuclear Planning Group (NPG), was established. It is composed of seven states selected on a rotating basis from among the member states of the NDAC. Britain, Canada, Germany, Italy, The Netherlands, Turkey and the United States are currently serving on the NPG. The principal role of the NPG is to do detailed work in the nuclear planning field under the policy guidance of the NDAC.

In the past it was impossible for the NATO nations to engage in meaningful discussion on nuclear planning because France was unwilling to accept any strategic doctrine not based on "massive retaliation." French withdrawal from the military structure of NATO makes possible exchange of views on various aspects of nuclear strategy. The Defense Planning Committee and the two newly organized bodies create a sense of participation in, and make possible contribution to, major policy decisions for large and small NATO states. This is particularly important for nations on whose territory the nuclear weapons themselves are deposited. Establishment of a strategy committee is not proliferation of atomic weapons, and thus the Soviet objection against German participation has no solid ground. The Soviet Union, to be sure, had raised objections against MLF and still opposes the setting up of any kind of multilateral atomic organization in NATO.

A political directorate of the major Western Powers within or outside NATO would not solve all problems. Agreement on policies would be greatly facilitated by continuous cooperation in several spheres. It is essential to organize high-level working groups for preparation of policy. Early coordination of major policies in planning is necessary. Inter-allied contingency planning in Washington during the Khrushchev-created Berlin crisis might serve as a precedent. In the first stage of that conflict there was much political disagreement among the major Western allies. Soon the German, French, and British ambassadors began meeting regularly with high officials of the State Department, and this group succeeded in framing a common policy. Their activity included contingency planning and systematic discussions of all important aspects of the Berlin question. In a similar way, representatives of the interested great powers should deal effectively with some specific political problems of the Western Alliance.

The fundamental cause of the conflict in Europe between the Soviet Union and the Western Alliance remains the artificial division of the Continent and the imposition of communist regimes on the East European nations. Normal relations between the Western Alliance and the Soviet Union are necessary for European security and world peace. But normalization cannot take place as long as Germany is partitioned and Europe divided against the will of the peoples involved. As long as the Kremlin does not recognize equality and self-determination for nations in the heart of Europe and pretends to consider fictions as facts, it is difficult to envisage a genuine settlement. "Stabilization" created by Soviet bayonets made necessary the installation of an iron curtain in the central part of the continent, the erection of a wall between East and West Berlin. Stabilization under these conditions is stabilization on top of a powder keg. Whether the conflict with China will influence the European policy of the Kremlin, and if so, when and how, only a prophet can predict. Optimistic speculations do not form realistic foundations for policy.

At the time NATO was founded the focus of danger was Europe. During the last decade communist expansion has changed direction, partly because of NATO's success and Europe's economic resurgence. The communist movement is expanding, naturally, in the direction of least resistance. Countries in the Indian Ocean, southern Asia, the Far East, Latin America, the Middle East, and Africa have become actual or potential targets of communist aggression and subversion. NATO powers should agree on cooperation with states which are regional powers on other continents. If leading NATO powers are unable or unwilling to agree on interpretation of some inportant movements and changes in world politics, NATO cannot respond. The mere existence of NATO, without agreement on fundamental issues, is not meaningful and may indeed prove to be counterproductive.

If the time-consuming and costly relocation of NATO organs and facilities diverted much energy which could have been used for important political problems, the French "go it alone" policy, on the other hand, gave occasion for a long-needed overhaul of the Alliance's structure. There have been not only political transformations but changes in military technology, which have made necessary the reappraisal of the Soviet threat in Europe. The lack of recurring crises and daily threats has created a typical atmosphere of wishful thinking. The Soviet Union has not made one single major concession, and quietly continues to build up its military strength in Eastern Europe.

The number and quality of divisions to be maintained on German soil depends on the appraisal of the Soviet threat. And at this point it is necessary to find ways of offsetting the exchange costs of the British and American troops in Germany. Britain has serious economic and financial problems which might make unavoidable a further reduction of the British Army of the Rhine. The United States has balance-of-payments difficulties, and Bonn was unable to meet conditions of the agreement concluded with Washinton concerning offset payments. The agreement provided for German purchase of American arms to offset the $675 million annual expenditure of the American Army in the Federal Republic. In view of European reluctance to participate adequately in defense of the Continent, Congressional pressure is mounting to reduce American troops in Germany. If the European nations would contribute more to Europe's defense, a reduction of American servicemen in Germany would be possible, which in turn would help the German undertaking to offset the exchange costs of the American Army in Germany.

The French policy of noncooperation immensely complicates the defense measures of NATO, particularly logistic problems and communications. France behaves almost like a neutral state, and divides Italy, Greece, and Turkey from the other NATO countries. General de Gaulle emphasized in his address of October 28, 1966, that "the servicemen, the materiel, the ships, the airplanes that will want to enter our country will do so by virtue of the authorizations that we will grant them for each separate case . . ." Installation of a space satellite system for NATO communications will improve the situation, but major inconveniences remain.

One may argue that the purposes of the Western nations differ in ways which make greater unity impossible. Can Western Europe organize itself as a unit without common purposes on such matters as Britain's relation to the Continent, United States relations to Europe, German reunification, and French claims to leadership, or without a shared policy toward China, the Soviet Union, and Eastern Europe? Discussion of these questions would necessitate volumes. It is sufficient to say here that the long-range interests of the Western states are the same and do not conflict with those of progressive mankind. Public debates of policy alternatives are the corollary of a democratic political system in both domestic and international relations, but in the Western Alliance differences are often exaggerated by public discussion, which is sometimes prejudicial to common understanding. It is easy to forget amid acrimonious public debates that few countries have as many common political interests as France and the United States. It is seldom recognized in public discussions that the French and British views are similar in respect to important aspects of European integration. Both nations prefer intergovernmental cooperation instead of supranationalism, though the boundaries between these categories have blurred. NATO is more than a military alliance, and with the proliferation of atomic weapons even military alliances have not become obsolete. Countries with some atomic capabilities know well that they cannot defend themselves against a super-power. The Soviet Union would not fear British atomic capabilities or the French *force de frappe* if these forces were isolated. In the Western Alliance, American willingness to protect Britain and France remains important for the foreseeable future. But it would be difficult for Washington to accept a situation in which Britain or France could drag the United States into an atomic war.

It is, indeed, disconcerting to think of Europe without NATO. A strong NATO made possible the economic miracle of Europe. Without political and military security, the regional economic organizations in Western Europe could not have developed their present strength. If security should disappear or dwindle, all these achievements may crumble. In European relations the revival of an old-time romantic nationalism in Gaullist thinking and action is disquieting. As nationalism is contagious, nationalistc tendencies and trends cannot limit themselves to France. Revival of nationalism by the Gaullists may boomerang in the same way as did the *gloire* of Napoleon III. A general aspiration to national greatness may contribute to dismantling or abandoning NATO and returning to the pre-1914 European system, which led to the suicidal folly of 1914-1918. Instead of disregarding the lessons of two world wars and some major factors in contemporary international politics, the French genius, we may hope, will help to lead Europe toward unification and Atlantic cooperation in harmony with the requirements of our age. If the intentions are clear and serious, a slower pace of progress would seem acceptable to most interested states.

In diplomacy there is a time for quick moves and a time for watchful waiting. NATO's crisis is urgent. Nevertheless, as the future of Europe is the more immediate question, initiative should come from Europeans. The European states should be able to make decisions about their plans. The United States is a strong country and can afford to wait. At the present stage of Atlantic affairs a reserved American attitude might be more productive than grandiose diplomatic initiatives. During travels in most Western European countries, this writer heard two major complaints against American diplomacy: its lack of leadership and its unwarranted over-activity. These complaints are, of course, ambivalent. In their exaggerated forms they are unjust or unfair, yet they are made time and again, even by some informed persons. Although many people believe that Europe simply cannot or will not act without American initiative, it is possible that the European nations are able to pour some clear water into the muddy channels of international politics. If they are dissatisfied with American leadership—or the lack of it—it is their turn to propose alternative courses.

Although most European nations expect American leadership, they are at the same time afraid of American moves which may affect their vital interests. They do not like to be pushed around and pressed, and are inclined to suspect hidden motives behind quite innocent American initiatives. They particularly resent unilateral announcements of American policy decisions in inter-Allied relations. Notably, the Europeans resented some of Secretary McNamara's speeches when he informed the American people (and incidentally, the Allied nations and the rest of the world) of some new American policies. His famous Ann Arbor address of June 16, 1962, on defense arrangements in NATO and especially on the importance of a strategy of centrally controlled response in atomic wars is a case in point. It is small consolation to allies that on some occasions the State Department was not properly consulted. Although such incidents are almost unavoidable in view of the worldwide effect of statements by American political leaders, more caution would be advisable. Diplomacy by surprise has been a perennial source of discord even between allies, and in addition, as mentioned, some European political circles are almost pathologically inclined to misinterpret American policy statements.

It is often forgotten by now that the Marshall Plan and NATO represented new and almost revolutionary ideas in trans-Atlantic relations. The United States has given abundant military and economic aid to Western Europe. It has assisted European rehabilitation and development in many ways, though all informed Americans knew from the very inception of this policy that a strong Europe would be a competitor of the United States. The idea of competition did not frighten Americans; it has been part of their philosophy and their idea of partnership. Pettiness is not an American characteristic, although the eagerness to achieve results may lead to impatience and the use of rough methods in international politics.

An affluent Western Europe has reached a political crossroads. It is clear that in the contemporary world such legal categories as federation and confederation have lost much of their traditional meaning. A close cooperation and fusion of certain governmental functions is necessary under new technological conditions, and this would not abolish the independent nationhood of European countries. Without combining resources, the European states cannot compete in basic research with the United States and the Soviet

Union (and later possibly with China), and in one or two decades Western Europe could become a technologically underdeveloped area.

What should be Europe's position in the world? The era of European colonialism has come irrevocably to an end. Europe is a small area and the Continent's resources are limited. For Europe "Unite or perish" is not an empty slogan. European states have to decide whether they will concentrate on the Continent and support cooperation there, or will turn toward the Atlantic and larger horizons. Not only the destiny of the Atlantic world but primarily their own future is at stake. With the possible exception of Gaullist France, most European countries are divided or uncertain and follow a policy of discreet silence on these important questions. The answers cannot be delayed indefinitely. Their attitude and decisions will influence inter-Atlantic relations and the direction of American foreign policy for decades. The United States will have to make choices. There is still a substantial desire in America for Atlantic partnership. Organized cooperation of NATO countries with less developed areas of the world would appeal to Americans and could become a great common enterprise for the benefit of all mankind. A period of persisting frustration may bring about important transformations in American foreign policy. Since the role of an unwelcome and abused suitor is not attractive, the American nation might turn inward and concentrate on the numerous problems of the vast North American continent. American shores face the Pacific as well as the Atlantic, and Washington also has traditional ties with Latin America.

The time has come for European states to make a decision about their aspirations, a choice about their role in world affairs. No outside nation can decide the issues for them.

ELEVEN

The World Task
of Western Diplomacy

Contemporary diplomacy operates in an unprecedented world environment. Diplomatic actions are similar to navigation on an uncharted sea full of reefs and icebergs. Still, an analysis of the operational conditions of Western diplomacy, may establish four major categories of states: (1) Western; (2) neutral and nonaligned; (3) communist countries; and (4) nations situated along the perimeter of communist countries and determined to maintain their freedom and independence. Different methods of diplomacy must be used toward states belonging to different categories, though there are numerous twilight zones. A number of states prefer to sit, so to speak, on the fence. Since this era of transition is characterized by dynamic changes, the political conditions and foreign policies of states may alter overnight. Diplomacy must be flexible in such situations. Western diplomacy has three basic objectives: (1) worldwide security; (2) expansion of freedom and welfare; and (3) harmonization of conflicting interests. What kind of institutional arrangements are necessary for these ends, and which diplomatic methods and techniques are most effective? Historical precedents do not indicate adequate answers. Since diplomacy is no longer restricted to contacts between chancelleries, one must consider many new and rapidly changing factors.

Western civilization has expanded in circles into the rest of the world. Industry and modernization have created similar problems in many regions. Great differences in national cultures, however, persist. The dynamics and possibilities of diplomacy change according to the stages and value systems of societies. Some failures of Western diplomacy in Africa and Asia have been partly caused by false assumptions about goals and means and about the social values of Asian and African peoples. Communist failures have similar causes in these areas. If the last decades have seen many new international institutions of universal, regional, and functional nature, events have demonstrated that better organization of international institutions cannot solve some issues which could lead to all-encompassing destruction, and so agreements must be on a deeper level of human aspirations and probably must come gradually.

Strengthening cooperation within the free world remains a major goal. Defense against communist aggression and subversion is still necessary, and for this purpose NATO and other defensive alliances are needed. Without the growing strength of Western Europe and NATO, the West cannot prevail in the gigantic turbulences of the late twentieth century.

Traditional methods of diplomacy are to be used primarily among states which accept comparable assumptions about goals and means—mainly the Atlantic world, the hub of Western civilization. On the deepest cultural level there is unity among the countries of Europe and the Americas. (Of course, Australia and New Zealand are culturally Western countries, despite their geographical location.) Cooperation, not competition, between Europe and the United States in Latin American affairs would be a specific realization of the Atlantic partnership and greatly would help to solve the problems in Latin American societies.

In diplomacy a strenuous effort is demanded of the democracies. A common understanding of the conditions of contemporary politics is a requisite for survival. Challenges arise not only from rapidly changing world conditions and from the flexible practices of dictatorships, but from internal quarrels within the democratic camp. One of the dangers is that some of the United States' partners may abuse their positions under the American atomic umbrella. Some European political leaders are convinced that there will be no war because of the overwhelming power of the United States, and are using this situation for nationalistic purposes. Conflicting national interests and different interpretations and applications of democratic principles in domestic and international relations are the causes of much friction. One of the consequences of democratic freedom is the lack of cooperation sometimes even among members of the Western alliance system. Whenever the diplomacy of the Western countries works at cross-purposes it is difficult to achieve political success.

In light of events of the last decades, most members of NATO realize how related are their freedom and security. A NATO that would be merely a strict military alliance, exposed to transformations in military technology and uncertainties of politics, could not fulfill its promise. In this interdependent world of ours, nations willing to fight together for their survival and way of life must coordinate their foreign policy, including some aspects of economic policy. Coordination does not mean creation of a Western voting machine in the United Nations, but the areas of cooperation should be established. Policies are necessary at least on fundamentals. From the long-range point of view, Europe and the United States are profoundly interdependent, and interdependence is great between Europe and the Americas in general. It is necessary to solve the question of how to secure greater European participation in an Atlantic process of policy-making—in the formulation and execution of general policies. Europeans should be made partners even in atomic matters. Participation of leading NATO countries in strategic planning represents progress and NATO's framework can be used for a variety of cooperative purposes.

It is difficult to change social attitudes and phobias, and consequently the growth of cooperation must be gradual. If European history does not offer many encouraging examples, at least the British and American inclination to compromise is a favorable influence. Traditions and practices of the Pan-American Conferences and the British Commonwealth are useful; they constitute major American and British contributions to NATO practices.

The European Communities and OECD present several new models for constructive cooperation which could be employed in trans-Atlantic relations. Assistance to developing countries could be closely coordinated through the OECD. The model of contingency planning during the Berlin crisis[1] could be used for some pressing political problems. Discussions between advocates of federalist and confederalist solutions may become exercises in futility, but the European Communities demonstrated that unification is possible in important areas of common interest without indulging in debates about national sovereignty. Trans-Atlantic organs could be created for handling selected problems. The conferences of NATO parliamentarians are symbols of solidarity among NATO nations. Cooperation of American congressmen with members of Canadian and European parliaments should develop more systematically. Increasing contacts between political leaders should develop the Atlantic partnership into a new political union, eventually to include an Atlantic Assembly, an Atlantic Political Authority, and an Atlantic system of international courts.

Then there is need for much more cultural cooperation. Contacts between European and American intellectuals should develop. The existence of an Atlantic civilization has been generally recognized, but a new Erasmus is needed to express the idea of a Euro-American community. This community can present a plurality of cultures because there is unity in the

[1] See above, pp. 154–55.

diversity. In politics unity does not mean unanimity—except in totalitarian regimes. Fundamental ideas associated with Western civilization are basic to NATO countries. Cultural coordination within NATO, especially cooperation in science, may be more important than coordination of defense expenditures, however necessary and important the latter may seem. The proposal of the Italian Government, in October 1966, for a technological "Marshall Plan" is a constructive move. If the European states are willing to make substantial public and private investments in research, American aid could bridge the scientific and technological gap between the United States and its European partners. The Italian plan suggests that similar technical aid should extend later to Eastern European and non-European countries.

Although fear was expressed that the new American administration in 1961 might change policy toward the Atlantic nations, in his message to NATO on February 15, 1961, President Kennedy not only pledged the United States to full military commitment to the Atlantic Alliance, but went further than the previous administration. He stressed Atlantic policies in nonmilitary fields and emphasized that the interest of the Atlantic Community transcended military cooperation. President Johnson has been continuing these policies.

Strengthening NATO is not only a Western interest; it is important for the whole noncommunist world and for the future of mankind. Europe, Canada, and the United States should close ranks in world affairs, while at the same time remaining open societies. Neither is cooperation between the two shores of the North Atlantic solely in the interest of the West; the security community in the North Atlantic should be the powerhouse of the world, the beacon of freedom pointing toward happier developments for the human race. Integration in the North Atlantic can foster freedom everywhere. Without a strong NATO it would be difficult for countries in Africa and Asia to follow a neutralist policy.

A special category in the present international system comprises states which have accepted political institutions and practices of Western derivation though their civilizations are not of Western origin. Some cooperate with the West; others are nonaligned. Japan, the Philippines, India, and some other Asian and African states have demonstrated that diplomacy can operate in such countries as in the Atlantic world.

Another category comprises nations of Asia and Africa, a sort of twilight zone. Some cooperate with communist countries. Others do not reject *rapprochment* with the West. Since many states in this group are characterized by lack of stability, if not of reliability, traditional methods of diplomacy are not effective. Most underdeveloped countries are willing to accept support from any source. Western representatives must proceed with extreme caution in this group because whimsical changes are possible.

The rapid multiplication of states in recent times has become a cause of confusion in international politics. Some fictions in the contemporary world are connected with this process. The European idea of a national state, and the high living standards in Western countries created the myth that similar results can come almost anywhere. This view overlooks the fact that in other areas the cultural background, value systems, and other important features of life are dissimilar. Geographic factors and climate remain important. The ideas of the nation state and self-determination simply are not applicable everywhere; some former colonies do not possess requisites of statehood. Chance factors of colonial conquest and the arbitrary boundaries of colonial powers can hardly be foundations for a state. The viability of the contemporary setting thus created in some parts of Africa and Asia is open to serious doubt from a long-range point of view.

Some of the new states are more geographic categories than nations or organized communities. The dreams of charismatic and unpredictable leaders with ambitions and expectations unrelated to the power of their country may further confuse the situation. In most new states the military forces play a political role and in many instances take over the government. Technical assistance, economic aid, or even solicited advice appears as intervention in domestic affairs. Under these conditions it is difficult to maintain a balance between the sensitivity to newly acquired sovereignty and the almost inevitable meddling—or appearance of meddling—in internal affairs. In view of the variety of such conditions only a sympathetic and flexible diplomacy can succeed.

On the farthest side of the spectrum are the communist states. In Stalin's time it was easy to characterize the communist bloc, but this is no longer the case, for communist unity has ceased to exist and the leaders of some communist countries now have greater freedom to pursue national policies. Antagonism between China and the USSR is a fundamental part of this change. Struggle between the two major communist powers is not necessarily favorable to the West; competition between China and the USSR might intensify aggressive communist policies, because both of them seek to demonstrate the effectiveness of their system. As for the East European states, they are trying to renew their ties with the rest of Europe and the United States. During a crisis their attitude might change. Western diplomacy should use realistic methods toward all communist countries.

Cooperation with communist states might, of course, become more possible in the future. President Johnson's initiatives in October 1966 were efforts in this direction. The East European countries, and to some extent even the USSR, belong to the European community of nations. A Europe extending to the Urals is not a wild dream, but there is a difficulty in that the Soviet Union is a Eurasian power with vital interests in Central Asia and the Far East. With prudence the United States and Western Europe will be able to work out differences with the European communist countries without major war, appeasement, or surrender. The timetable of such developments is uncertain and setbacks are inevitable. A firm American attitude and coordination of Western policies are conditions of success. The enormous economic strength of the Western powers has not been used as leverage toward the communist states or in the underdeveloped countries because of lack of common Western policy.

As long as the communist states do not change their political philosophy and practices, the Western nations should give all necessary aid and assistance to countries exposed to aggression and subversion, particularly along the perimeter of the communist world. The special position of neutral states should be respected. Support should go primarily to governments able to carry out social reforms and raise living standards. In many developing countries democracy in the Western sense is not an immediate alternative. The important criterion of Western support should be social justice in a political framework which would eventually allow people to rule themselves in harmony with their own traditions.

As the world approaches the 1970s, it is possible to question the continued validity of some of the postwar policies. When the Truman Doctrine was proclaimed the United States had an atomic monopoly. This situation gradually changed when the Soviet Union also acquired a thermonuclear capability, although the massive American nuclear power retains its meaning to the present time. Soviet policy leapfrogged Western defense lines outside of Europe, and the Soviet Union gained influence in the Middle East, Southern Asia, and Africa. While Dean Acheson established close cooperation and an alliance system mainly with highly industrial European states, John Foster Dulles concluded alliances, sometimes in partnership with Britain and France, with underdeveloped countries in order to contain communism in Asia. The major theater of American-Soviet confrontation until the early 1950s was Europe. Although Europe has remained the decisive area of contention between the superpowers, the struggle has become worldwide. Some of the non-European alliances have proved of dubious value and the universal application of the Truman Doctrine could lead to dispersion of American strength. Developments during the last decade have shown the unsuitability of the Truman Doctrine whenever a majority of people of a nation or would-be nation is unable or unwilling to make the effort and sacrifice to fight communist subversion. Communist actions are often connected with nationalist movements and this combination creates confusion.

The appearance of Communist China as a major factor in world affairs has complicated the situation. China's thermonuclear and missile capabilities might radically change the world balance of power. In general, Communist China has followed a cautious policy in military matters. Her attitude in the Formosa Strait in 1958 and in the Vietnamese war are cases in point. Chinese propaganda and subversion have been growing and Chinese domestic political developments are full of explosive elements. China is a world in itself. Although Washington, London, Paris, and Moscow may desire friendly relations with her, unilateral goodwill is not sufficient. As the economic and social problems of many new nations cannot be solved within the foreseeable future, it is possible that in a decade or so an exasperated and fully armed China might take over leadership of the revolutionary forces of the world. The almost complete lack of freedom of speech in China, coupled with indoctrination and isolation of the Chinese nation, constitutes a great danger. It would be of utmost importance to establish as many channels of communication as possible with the Chinese people. In all probability, Communist China's hostility toward all Western states will remain a major obstacle to development of a cooperative world society. China's participation would be particularly important in negotiations connected with disarmament, banning the spread of nuclear weapons, and stabilizing peaceful conditions in Southeast Asia. A policy aiming at China's isolation is unrealistic and counterproductive.

Strong desire for social change and economic progress has generated new trends in world politics and created special responsibilities for the richest nation. American diplomacy has had to expand its activities to economic and technical fields, and traditional diplomacy can offer little guidance. In our time societies which have been static for many centuries desire a better fate. A longing for change has become a strong political motive, particularly in the developing countries. The leaders of new nations realize that political independence is meaningless unless they can fight poverty, ignorance, and other social plights. The advantage of communist propaganda is that in a world filled with desire for change, communism offers unlimited and often unscrupulous promises, an organizational pattern, and a timetable for action. It presents the ideal of a system in which man's wants will be satisfied and human dignity prevail. Western states should fight communist propaganda in the realm of ideas. Even poor people are sensitive about their dignity, and the new nations are yearning for ideas. Many individuals in the new nations, faced with the breakdown of their cultures, are searching for a sense of identity. The Western nations should recognize the critical situation and call the bluff of communism philosophically as well as politically.

Since the proclamation of the Point Four Program in 1949, the developing countries, particularly the new states, have come to expect American economic aid and technical assistance as a matter of course, and as the balance of terror has begun to limit political maneuvers, the importance of economic diplomacy has increased. Leading Western nations and Japan now have an instrument—the Development Assistance Committee of the OECD—for coordination of their technical assistance programs.[2] Meanwhile, a frustrated American public has become dissatisfied with the "ingratitude" of nations helped by the United States in critical times, and the usefulness of foreign aid has been questioned by powerful forces in Congress. One should distinguish sharply between economic aid to Western Europe and aid programs for developing countries. The success of the European Recovery Program may have created the illusion that economic aid will have beneficial effects everywhere, irrespective of the stage of development of the recipient countries.

Few Americans notice that the United States has contributed to the creation of a new world, the forces of which one cannot channel, let alone control, by obsolete diplomatic techniques. New ideas, methods, and agreements among Western allies and developing nations are necessary for handling the awesome problems of a rapidly evolving world society. Aid should be given increasingly on a regional basis and channelled through the World Bank and other international agencies.

As the strongest world power, the United States is confronted with dilemmas in most parts of the globe. In many cases choices are not between good and evil, but between the devil and the deep blue sea. American diplomacy is blamed for unwelcome developments in numerous countries, irrespective of the merit of specific diplomatic actions or inactions. Foreign policy, however, is not a popularity contest. Diplomacy is the art of the possible. In international affairs it is usually better to be respected than loved.[3]

[2] See above, p. 102.

[3] See for specific problems of American foreign policy, the following Spectrum books published by Prentice-Hall, Englewood Cliffs, N.J.: Willard L. Thorp, ed., *The United States and the Far East*, 2nd ed. (1962); Herbert L. Matthews, ed., *The United States and Latin America*, 2nd ed. (1963); John Sloan Dickey, ed., *The United States and Canada* (1964); Georgiana G. Stevens, ed., *The United States and the Middle East* (1964); Marian D. Irish, ed., *World Pressures on American Foreign Policy* (1966); Bernard K. Gordon, *The Dimensions of Conflict in Southeast Asia* (1966). See for the complexities of foreign policy, Roy C. Macridis, ed., *Foreign Policy in World Politics*, 2nd ed. (1962); Joseph E. Black and Kenneth W. Thompson, *Foreign Policies in a World of Change* (New York: Harper & Row, Publishers, Inc., 1963).

The ambitions and emotions of developing nations are worthy of respect. But Western policy-makers must consider the facts of life. It is probable that the population explosion will make a rising living standard difficult in many countries—no matter how much economic aid those countries receive. Even if the economic growth would be more rapid in developing than in developed countries, which is not the case, it would take "more than 200 years for the two average income levels to be the same." [4] Western nations should open the gates of opportunity to enable these countries to benefit from Western technological experience. But they must be taught realistically. The less fortunate nations cannot expect to follow the same path as Western nations. Differences between the temperate zones and the often overpopulated tropical zones will remain.

Stupendous progress was possible during the past centuries of the "modern era"—everything since the time of the Renaissance and Reformation and the rise of nation states—because Western political institutions increasingly have secured freedom, including freedom of inquiry. Can this continue today? What, indeed, is the problem? Western civilization is not a geographical idea, and its doom is not determined—as some cyclical-minded historians predict. Western ideas, values, and methods have expanded over the world. This expansion is not altogether a triumphant march. Jingo-nationalist ideas, and particularly totalitarian Nazism and communism, have been harmful aspects of Western civilization. Identification of the West with material well-being and technology, power and imperialism, has contributed to the loss of respect which Western nations have suffered in recent decades. Still, the fact of plenty is rapidly becoming apparent and attractive. The same people who curse the West would like to have the material advantages of Western civilization.

The human race, one might say, has reached a crossroad. Or—to change the figure of speech—we may now be on the threshold of great international change. The emergence of the *tiers monde* is the beginning of a new period of history. The present era is a time of enormous physical plenty for many of the peoples of the world. For the first time in history not only a small circle of privileged people but even the ordinary man can enjoy the comforts of life—primarily, but not exclusively, in the northern hemisphere. In some regions the revolution of rising expectations is being threatened by waves of frustration rolling in catastrophic dimensions. The underdeveloped southern part of the globe has formidable problems. In some international conferences the division of states is not so much east-west as

---

[4] Cf. Thorkil Kristensen, "The Western Industrialized Nations and Developing Countries," *The OECD Observer* (December 1964), p. 4.

it is north-south, and this direction possibly foreshadows new political groupings.

For the foreseeable future two threats remain. One is the changed nature of war. The other is the expansion of tyrannical political systems: dictatorship of the few, and institutionalized insecurity and servitude for the majority. Democracies can be weakened through unscrupulous political warfare, and even their destruction might be possible through surprise nuclear attack. Much depends on the development of nuclear weaponry and the spread of atomic weapons. Although both superpowers are aware of the suicidal aspects of a nuclear war and neither wishes to fight the other, their leaders might be conditioned by historical patterns and start a war because of misunderstanding. The possibility of mutual destruction is an effective deterrent, and as long as the "balance of terror" prevails between the US and the USSR, a surprise attack is not likely. At the present stage of human development a world community exists primarily in a negative form as a community of fear in the face of thermonuclear devastation. A war fought with microbiological and chemical weapons can have even more terrible effects. This community of fear may help to develop constructive ideas and methods for settlement of conflicts, realization of peaceful change, and eventually cooperation for the universal good.

A universal world order is a long-range aspiration. It seems that in this thoroughly divided and confused society of states, a genuine international order must be preceded by consensus-building. Although the difficulties are astronomical, without understanding on ends and means there is no community; and without a community feeling there is little basis for a worldwide political authority and legal system. That an international organization alone cannot change or even influence the flow of ideas and the course of major political events has been amply demonstrated by the League of Nations and the United Nations. If the latter has proved resilient, its operations are limited by external political factors. If some of its successes are encouraging, progress in specific fields cannot eliminate basic difficulties in the contemporary world. A political system, let alone a system of law, can be established only in a community which has the same general views of some fundamental principles governing human relations. Efficient organizations may preclude or minimize some sources of conflict. Other sources are the product of political and moral disagreement. Indeed, science, technology, and organization may make such problems more awesome and yet be able to contribute little to their solution. All political and legal systems have philosophical and moral considerations and assumptions, and the international order or community is no exception. Gradual development of a common moral standard is necessary for survival. A new international climate is needed for acceptance of common moral standards and a novel international system in which law can replace force. Changes—primarily in the minds of men—are imperative.

Serious moral issues are connected with major policies, particularly with unrestricted warfare and with the use of thermonuclear weapons.[5] However, day-to-day foreign policy decisions seldom raise moral issues directly. If two military dictatorships fight a civil war, the question of support of one of them is influenced more by national interest than by moral considerations.

The rapid progress of natural sciences and technology has changed the prospects and expectations of humanity. Technical advances, modern means of communication, and greatly improved functional organizations do not solve fundamental problems of world society. Technological progress may make the solution of political issues more difficult because it creates physical proximity between antagonistic and mutually envious states and state systems. Despite some United Nations success, difficulties in international politics have persisted and even increased since 1945 because it has not been possible to clarify some issues that divide mankind. Genuine progress is necessarily slow as long as nations are in the dark about developments and thinking in other parts of the world. Astronauts can circle the globe in eighty minutes, but hundreds of millions of human beings have no freedom of communication with their fellow men. The brotherhood of man cannot come unless and until freedom of communication can dispel false information and misunderstandings. The common good appears differently to various groups of the human family, and clarification is hardly possible without freedom of inquiry and an exchange of views. But in many countries the mass media of communication are not for the exchange of ideas and information, but for promoting indoctrination to serve the interests of power.

Despite the difficulties connected with international activities in a shrinking but ideologically divided world, the collective interests of mankind are overwhelming. All nations are interested in survival and peaceful develop-

---

[5] See for the role of moral problems in international affairs, Martin J. Hillenbrand, *Power and Morals* (New York: Columbia University Press, 1951); Earnest W. Lefever, *Ethics and United States Foreign Policy* (New York: Meridian Books, Inc., 1957); William Clancy, ed., *The Moral Dilemma of Nuclear Weapons* (New York: The Church Peace Union, 1961); Kenneth W. Thompson, *Christian Ethics and the Dilemmas of Foreign Policy* (Durham, N.C.: Duke University Press, 1959); Kenneth W. Thompson, *The Moral Issue in Statescraft* (Baton Rouge: Louisiana State University Press 1966); Paul Ramsey, *The Limits of Nuclear War* (New York: The Council on Religion and International Affairs, 1963); N. Politis, *La Morale Internationale* (Neuchâtel: Editions de la Baconnière, 1943).

ments. No nation can provide security for itself. A rising living standard is one of the bases for cooperation. Human dignity, charity, and mutual understanding are most important for the unity of mankind. Nations need a dream of the future world more than they need the amenities of our industrial age. Understanding of the purposes of man and of important problems of life is a preliminary condition of political and economic cooperation. The mainstream of history will be influenced by the ideas of human dignity and freedom and the intellectual currents that have flowered in Graeco-Roman and Judaeo-Christian civilization. These ideas have made possible modern science, the industrial revolution, the harnessing of nuclear energy, and the exploration of outer space. We are on the threshold of greater transformations. The Western world is going along this road and the rest of the human family is catching up. We may approach a golden age. Men of all religions, races, and political persuasions must close ranks, because the globe is becoming every day a smaller place where human failure might make life uncomfortable, if not impossible.

Mankind then is in a quandary. Although man has invaded the cosmos, he has been unable to solve political and social problems. Understanding and cooperation between political leaders and social and physical scientists have become necessities. We have to find new ways and means to survive.

Understanding the requirements of our age is the first step toward adjustment of our thinking and attitudes in political matters. The need for new diplomatic methods and practices cannot be overemphasized. These represent a bridge between the present and the future, in a period of transition. Old conventions and traditions of international conduct have their merits, but they cannot be universally applied in our time. New diplomatic approaches should lead to modern international institutions and contribute to the creation of an entirely new, more cooperative world system. In the past diplomacy has often secured a shaky peace in periods of danger, which in some instances lasted for a long time indeed. This peace-preserving function has remained a primary task of contemporary diplomacy.

Although the state of world affairs may encourage pessimism, many developments encourage confidence in the final victory of man over "things." Political and social organizations and legal institutions must come into harmony with realities all over the world—a difficult process, because in many countries the proper state of mind does not exist. Public acceptance of political and social changes remains slow. In the course of history reasonable men could not always prevail, and "things" took over. But history now has outrun the conventional objectives of foreign policy. General suicide is in nobody's interest. Modern science and technology make possible such cooperative works as desalting sea water, influencing weather conditions, controlling disease, developing a world communications-satellite system, and exploring outer space, the depths of the sea, and the nucleus of the earth. Such ventures could become undertakings of mankind, which would create a feeling of unity—a new basis for diplomacy in the closing decades of the twentieth century. Through such endeavors, Ernest Renan's definition of the nation—to have done great things together and to desire to continue—should find a new application. William Faulkner expressed this sort of optimism in his speech in acceptance of the Nobel Prize in Literature:

> I decline to accept the end of man. . . . I believe that man will not merely endure: he will prevail. He is immortal not because he alone among creatures has an inexhaustible voice but because he has a soul, a spirit capable of compassion and sacrifice and endurance.

These words are lights for diplomacy in the struggle toward a more peaceful world.

Index